TEEN
SMOKING

Other books in the At Issue series:

TEEN
SMOKING

Hayley Mitchell Haugen, *Book Editor*

Daniel Leone, *President*
Bonnie Szumski, *Publisher*
Scott Barbour, *Managing Editor*
Helen Cothran, *Senior Editor*

San Diego • Detroit • New York • San Francisco • Cleveland
New Haven, Conn. • Waterville, Maine • London • Munich

For more information, contact
Greenhaven Press
27500 Drake Rd.
Farmington Hills, MI 48331-3535
Or you can visit our Internet site at http://www.gale.com

LIBRARY OF CONGRESS CATALOGING-IN-PUBLICATION DATA
Teen smoking / Hayley Mitchell Haugen, book editor.
p. cm. — (At issue)
Includes bibliographical references and index.
ISBN 0-7377-1971-0 (lib. : alk. paper) — ISBN 0-7377-1972-9 (pbk. : alk. paper)
1. Teenagers—Tobacco use. 2. Smoking. 3. Tobacco habit—Prevention.
I. Haugen, Hayley Mitchell, 1968– . II. At issue (San Diego, Calif.)
HV5745.T43 2004
362.29'6'0835—dc21   2003054041

Printed in the United States of America

Contents

Introduction

Deaths caused by smoking have reached epidemic proportions. In the United States alone, 430,000 people die annually from smoking-related illnesses such as cancers and lung disease. Stephen Jay, chair of the Department of Public Health at Indiana University School of Medicine, states that tobacco's "human toll far exceeds the Black Death of the 14th century, the global influenza pandemic of 1918–19, and the modern tragedy of HIV-AIDS."

Health care advocates, concerned about tobacco-related deaths and illnesses, have worked tirelessly to discourage cigarette smoking in the United States through education campaigns that warn the public about the potential health dangers of tobacco use. A particular target for these antismoking messages is teen smokers. According to 2001 data collected by the American Cancer Society, teen smoking rates have gradually decreased since their rapid rise throughout the 1980s and most of the 1990s. Despite this encouraging decrease in the number of teen smokers, however, approximately three thousand teens still start smoking each day. One-third of these teens will die prematurely of a smoking-related disease.

One hotly debated issue in the effort to prevent teen smoking is the role that tobacco industry advertisements play in influencing teens' decisions to begin smoking. Health care professionals view the tobacco industry—often referred to as "Big Tobacco"—as a rich, adversarial force to be reckoned with. In 2002, for example, the United States spent approximately $800 million on various tobacco-control initiatives, including antismoking campaigns aimed at teen smokers. Big Tobacco, however, spent nearly $8 billion on tobacco marketing. Such aggressive tobacco marketing is worrisome to those working to prevent teen smoking, since many tobacco advertisements often reach a youth-oriented audience.

The case of the cool, smoking camel

As evidence of tobacco advertisements' negative impact on American youths, antismoking groups often point to R.J. Reynolds's Joe Camel advertising campaign, which debuted in 1988. Joe Camel was a cool, sunglass-sporting, leather-jacket-wearing cartoon character featured on billboards and in magazine ads. According to one 1991 study published in the *Journal of the American Medical Association*, Joe Camel was as easily recognized by six-year-olds as Mickey Mouse. It was not long before this highly recognizable figure began to attract young smokers. By 1995, 13.3 percent of teen smokers smoked Camel cigarettes, a fact that led antismoking groups to accuse R.J. Reynolds of marketing tobacco specifically to minors.

Some commentators reject the claim that such advertising leads to more teen smoking. Social ecologist Mike Males, for example, notes that although the Joe Camel campaign may have influenced teens' choice of cigarette brand, it did not necessarily increase the number of teen smokers. In fact, Males says in his book *Smoked: Why Joe Camel Is Still Smiling*, "more [tobacco industry] ad/promo spending is correlated, though not significantly, with slightly *lower* rates of teen smoking." And according to one survey by the National Institute of Drug Abuse (NIDA), teen smoking actually decreased more rapidly in the five years following Joe Camel's debut than the five years prior. Regardless of these statistics, the harsh criticism R.J. Reynolds received as a result of its Joe Camel campaign led the company to eventually abandon the icon in 1997.

Lawsuits against Big Tobacco

R.J. Reynolds's discontinuation of the Joe Camel campaign in 1997 did not decrease criticism against the company. As a result of unrelated litigation in the same year, R.J. Reynolds and other tobacco giants were required by the courts to release documents that proved that the industry had made a practice of illegally targeting teen smokers through their ad campaigns. In addition, the tobacco industry was found guilty of suppressing evidence of known health hazards linked to smoking.

In light of these findings, 1997 became an expensive year for the tobacco industry. It settled numerous class-action liability suits that found the industry culpable of knowingly contributing to smoking-related deaths and illnesses. The state of Florida settled its suit with the industry for $11 billion; Minnesota for $6 billion; and Mississippi for $3.4 billion. In yet another class-action suit, sixty thousand flight attendants settled their case with the tobacco industry for $300 million.

By far the most significant tobacco industry settlement, the Master Settlement Agreement (MSA) of 1998, held the four largest tobacco companies liable for $206 billion, to be paid over a period of twenty-five years, to compensate forty-six U.S. states for tobacco-related health costs. Big Tobacco also pledged to fund a $1.5 billion, five-year antismoking campaign, to abide by marketing restrictions that prohibit the use of cartoon characters in ads, and to ban large-scale outdoor advertising, in addition to other restrictions.

Some critics of the MSA argue that these restrictions on Big Tobacco are not sufficient to address the problem of teen smoking. While the agreement includes restrictions on youth access to tobacco, for example, it does not include restrictions on point-of-sale advertising or vending machine sales of tobacco products. In *The Fight Against Big Tobacco*, Mark Wolfson notes that critics of the plan are concerned that the MSA "contains no 'lookback' provisions, which would levy financial penalties on tobacco companies if specified reductions in underage tobacco use are not met."

Tobacco advertising is not the only issue affecting teen smoking

Despite the Master Settlement Agreement and the ensuing ban on advertising tobacco products to youths, many antismoking groups today maintain that Big Tobacco is still continuing to promote smoking to teens and children through the sponsorship of sporting events and concerts; advertisements in magazines that are geared toward eighteen- to twenty-four-year-olds but are often read by younger readers; and product placements in films rated as low as "G" for young viewers. Other antismoking advocates, however, contend that the role of cigarette advertising in influencing teen smokers has been overestimated and that antismoking campaigns should instead focus on other factors that encourage teen smoking, such as peer or parental influences.

These differing viewpoints are reflected in *At Issue: Teen Smoking*, along with other perspectives from health care advocates, educators, tobacco industry supporters, lawmakers, parents, and teens. In addition to the controversies surrounding tobacco advertising, topics for debate and discussion include the reasons teens smoke and the best ways to help them quit or prevent them from starting.

1

Teen Smoking: An Overview

Susan Dominus

Susan Dominus has worked as an assistant editor at Glamour *magazine, a feature editor and contributor for* The American Lawyer *magazine, and senior editor at* New York Magazine.

Each day more than two thousand youths try cigarettes for the first time. Some teens think smoking looks sexy or cool; others hope cigarettes will help them lose weight or make them seem independent. Having parents who smoke is also likely to influence a teen's decision in favor of smoking. With their busy schedules, many teens today suffer from similar stresses and anxieties as adults. Many turn to cigarettes for the same reason adults do; nicotine has the same calming effect on teen smokers as it does on adults. Cigarette advertising also encourages teens to smoke. Cigarette ads are designed to make smoking appealing, and many are geared for the teen audience in particular. Despite the efforts of antismoking campaigns and legislation enacted to make cigarettes less readily available to teens, many teen smokers are already addicted to nicotine.

The town of Rye, in New York's Westchester County, has a small-town sweetness to it, with an old-fashioned amusement park and a pretty, tree-lined main street. TD's Rye Smoke Shop, located on a central corner, is one of the best-preserved throwbacks to past times, a dimly lit but homey place where kids clamor for dime candy, licorice, and dipsticks.

TD's also sells cigarettes and cigars, though not to kids under 18, in accordance with New York State law. But that doesn't stop them from finding cigarettes elsewhere. Across the street at Starbucks, almost every afternoon, you see 14-, 15-, and 16-year-olds approach one another, asking for a smoke, for a lighter, for another cigarette. It's their way of saying hello, of gaining entree. "Everyone smokes," says Candace, an open-faced 17-year-old enjoying a sunny Friday afternoon on a shop stoop. "Kids in every clique—jocks, preps, goths. . . ."

Compared with drug or alcohol abuse, smoking may seem like the least of a parent's worries, a relatively controlled way for a child to let off some steam or exert her independence. And yet, smoking is one of the riskiest behaviors a kid can indulge in—it's just that the life-threatening

Susan Dominus, "Teens and Tobacco: A Love Story," *Good Housekeeping*, vol. 235, November 2002, p. 118. Copyright © 2002 by Susan Dominus. Reproduced by permission.

dangers don't stare a parent in the face right away. With every study, the news gets more grim. The younger a child starts smoking, for example, the more likely she is to end up with lung cancer, according to recent research from the Harvard School of Public Health—and not just because of the cumulative impact. The younger the smoker, says the study, the more stubborn the carcinogenic buildup that damages DNA and is a precursor to tumor growth; the change starts early and is irreversible.

More than one quarter of all teens say they smoke today. That number is slightly lower than it was five years ago. Yet each day, over 2,000 young people still dabble with smoking for the first time, and a substantial number of them will eventually die of a smoking-related disease. Young adults ages 18 to 24 are also the fastest-growing group of smokers.

Why light up?

So why do kids light up in the first place?

"Some friends of mine in seventh grade just said, 'Why don't we try it?'" says Paul, now a sophomore. His arm draped around Candace, he's wearing cargo pants and is halfway through a cigarette. He's going to be handsome one day, but right now he's skinny, with a rash of acne across his chin only partly disguised by some sparse stubble. He holds a pack of Camels prominently in his hand, like a talisman, turning it upside down, tapping it on the sidewalk like a toy. "I thought, Well, if it's so bad for you, and people do it anyway, there must be something really great about it, right?"

Paul is in a band that's playing later at the town rec hall, and whenever a friend walks by, he calls after him, "See you tonight, right?" Every so often he coughs, making a harsh hacking sound. "I'm the sickliest kid," he admits. But he shrugs when asked if he's worried about getting seriously sick in the future, possibly as a result of smoking. "I'm not afraid of cancer," he says. "I believe in living fast and dying young."

"It's horrible," says Candace. "But there's something so sexy about cigarettes." Her face gets dreamy. "I like it when guys light a cigarette with a match and then flick it away. It's so destructive—so bad boy."

> *"The effects of nicotine in raising mood and lowering anxiety are important for teens as well as for adults."*

A familiar association. In fact, teenagers smoke for some of the same reasons they always have: It looks cool and they identify it with rebellion. And knowing the risks, as kids now do, may only enhance the appeal. But there's more to it than that. In addition to the old temptations to smoke, kids today have a constellation of reasons that are unique to their generation.

Ever since the introduction of Virginia Slims in 1968, the tobacco industry has lured women with the promise that they could smoke their way to a thinner body. Young women worrying about their weight is nothing new, but the worrying begins earlier these days, fed by a barrage of media images. "I see kids experiencing this pressure to look like the successful people they see on TV, which for teenage girls, means the actresses on *Friends*, for example," says Michael Levine, a professor of psychology at Ohio's Kenyon College, who specializes in body image and eating disorders. The current fashions for young girls—baby tees, belly-baring halter tops, spaghetti-strap tanks—flaunt more of their bodies, which means more self-scrutiny and, inevitably, self-criticism sooner. Given these pressures, smoking may seem like a quick fix, a diet trick that girls are afraid to go without.

Lisa, a blue-eyed, honey-haired girl with someone's phone number scrawled in pink on her arm, swings by the stoop, Gap bag in hand, to say hi to Candace. "She smokes, and she's an athlete," says Candace, pointing at Lisa. In fact, Lisa explains, she just stopped playing basketball this year and found herself adrift. For comfort, "it was either food or cigarettes, and I chose cigarettes because I didn't want to get gigantic."

Her parents, both overweight and longtime smokers, recently lost more than 20 pounds each. They dieted, "but the smoking helped," according to their daughter. "They're afraid to quit, because they're afraid they'll gain the weight back." Given that the children of smokers are more likely to smoke themselves, Lisa's habit—by now, an addiction, she says with resignation—almost seems inevitable.

Parents' influence on teen smokers

Rather than trying to free girls from concerns about their looks, a number of state-supported antismoking campaigns advise parents to work that angle—and point out that smoking, while it may depress weight, also leads to more wrinkles and sallow skin. "I try to appeal to my daughter's vanity," says Megan Powers, a mother of four from Westchester County, referring to her oldest daughter, Colette. "I tell her, 'It makes your teeth yellow, it makes your fingers yellow.'"

The family's relationship to cigarettes is a complicated one. Colette, now 20, started smoking with friends about four years ago, but as she puts it, "My dad always smoked, so my parents couldn't get too mad." Ironically, Colette says that smoking actually helped her to create a bond with her father. During a difficult time for the family—she and her parents were arguing constantly over her failure to call when she stayed out late—Colette says there was only one time when she could open up to her father: when the two lit up together on the porch. Though both parents disapproved of her smoking, her mother sensed that it wouldn't help to force the issue. "Was I going to ground her for smoking?" Megan Powers asks rhetorically. "No."

In the past six months or so, Colette has been getting along better with her parents and is happier overall; though still living at home, she's attending college nearby. She hasn't given up smoking yet, but she's smoking less, she says, and she intends to quit soon—partly because she's noticed she has less energy, but also because she's seen through her father how hard it can be to shake the habit once you get older.

Megan Powers's decision to tread lightly with Colette may have been the best tactic under the circumstances. Taking harsh measures with teens can easily backfire, according to Cheryl Healton, president of the American Legacy Foundation, a nonprofit public health organization. Healton suggests playing on a teenager's natural altruism instead. "Point out that even though they may not care about themselves, they're also hurting their friends, even their pets," she says, citing a study that found that cats in smokers' homes were far more likely to develop cancer than cats in tobacco-free homes. "And teenagers also like to get mad, so give them something to get mad about—those tobacco executives whose interest is not your kids' health but their own wealth."

A parent has to be creative, she adds, and tailor an approach for her own kid. Ruth Wooden's son, John, now 18, started to smoke when he was 14, stopped when he was 15, then picked up the habit again at 16. A former smoker herself, Wooden told John how incredibly hard it had been for her to quit, "and the amazing feeling of power I got when I finally did." Her son, she says, "responded to the challenge." When he was 17, around the same time he started taking fitness seriously, John quit again. "He says he can't imagine ever smoking again," his mother maintains.

Teens' reasons for smoking have changed

At 2:20 on an uncharacteristically warm Thursday afternoon in Seattle, the crowd lining the driveway of a sprawling high school is thinning out, leaving behind a core group of 20 or so kids. There's something clannish-looking about them as they bow toward each other almost ritualistically, lighting one another's cigarettes, then stand up and blow smoke off to the side. "Yeah, we're the popular clique," says Kristin, a freckled girl in a striped halter top, her strawberry-blond hair pulled back in a ponytail. "You start smoking to be cool, and then you get addicted," she says matter-of-factly. Her ex-boyfriend, now close buddy Rob, a tall varsity football and basketball player who also smokes, nods in agreement.

There are thousands of miles between home-of-grunge Seattle and New York's Rye, and Kristin's view of cigarettes seems to reflect that distance. Asked if weight control has anything to do with why she smokes, she looks like she's been asked whether she thinks smoking might make her turn purple. "No," she says, "that's not really our thing here."

Kristin argues that kids smoke because they're so independent—which means more responsibility and stress, less parental control. "I tell my parents what I'm doing, not the other way around," she says. "I go to high school, I'm going to night school for college credit, and I have a waitressing job; I earn my own spending money. Sometimes you just need a cigarette." Kristin is not unusual: 55 percent of 12th graders now work three hours or more on a typical school day, according to one survey. Combining a job with the typical pressures of school and adolescence boosts a student's stress level; the extra income gives them the cash they need to buy the cigarettes that seem to calm them down.

Nicotine relieves anxiety in adults and has the same calming effect on kids. "Twenty-five years ago, we thought the main reason kids smoked was because of peer pressure," says Edwin Fisher, Ph.D., a professor of psychology, medicine, and pediatrics at Washington University, in St. Louis. "We now understand that the effects of nicotine in raising mood and lowering anxiety are important for teens as well as for adults."

Although every era has its anxieties, the stresses on the average teenager today seem more numerous—and possibly more disturbing. "I think there's a sense of our world feeling less safe for everyone, but teens feel those shifts more acutely," says Nadine Kaslow, a professor and chief psychologist at Emory University, in Atlanta, who specializes in adolescence and families. "Yes, there are more teens working, but there's also a higher divorce rate, more violence that they see on television and in movies, and absolutely more violence in everyday life. And kids don't have good ways to regulate their feelings. So they turn to cigarettes for that."

Some antitobacco activists pay close attention to studies that identify kids who are at high risk for smoking, so they can throw them off course. Kids suffering from depression, for example, are more receptive to tobacco advertising and more likely to experiment, according to researchers at the University of Pennsylvania/Georgetown University Transdisciplinary Tobacco Use Research Center. And several studies have established that kids who have attention deficit disorder are twice as likely to start smoking as those who don't. In one of the more aggressive measures under way, Timothy Wilens, M.D., director of substance-abuse services in the pediatric psychopharmacology unit at Massachusetts General Hospital, in Boston, has started a trial in which kids with attention deficit disorder who don't already smoke are prescribed Zyban—which can function as either an antidepressant or a smoking-cessation medication—to stop them from ever starting. "It could have a great combination effect," Dr. Wilens says.

The advertising battle

In 1998, the major tobacco companies reached a settlement with the attorneys general of 46 states; among the provisions was a ban on cigarette advertising on billboards and on marketing directly to kids—including in magazines read primarily by young people. But despite the restrictions, tobacco marketing inexorably marches on, with manufacturers ingeniously slipping ads into new places sure to target brand-conscious kids. "When the billboards came down, you saw increases in promotions at places like convenience stores," says Danny McGoldrick, director of research at the Washington, D.C.–based Campaign for Tobacco-Free Kids. "We know that 75 percent of kids visit convenience stores at least once a week, so they're still getting bombarded." According to the Centers for Disease Control and Prevention, cigarette displays appear in 92 percent of the stores located in communities around public schools; other recent polls have found kids more likely than adults to be exposed to cigarette advertising.

But the antismoking lobby has grown more sophisticated about its own marketing techniques, creating television ads using kids to show kids that smoking isn't cool—rather than adults lecturing them about the dangers. The American Legacy Foundation's Truth Campaign, for example, created a series of television ads that appeal to kids' sense of the subversive, pitting them against the industry suits trying to make a buck at their expense. The foundation placed the commercials nationally, choosing edgy programming—"MTV or wrestling, not Seventh Heaven," says American Legacy's Healton. The Truth Campaign spots have started to make an impression, according to the Research Triangle Institute, which conducted a phone survey of 15,000 randomly selected teens and queried them about which commercials they'd seen, as well as about their smoking habits. (The findings were published in the *American Journal of Public Health*.)

Along with savvy advertising, hard-hitting legislative policies are chipping away at kids' inclination to smoke: In Florida, teens under 18 caught with cigarettes may find themselves losing their driver's license or facing steep fines, rather than just getting a warning from Mom. And in states like New York and California, legislators have recently imposed steep taxes on cigarettes—New York now charges $7 a pack, the highest price in the nation—which is expected to inhibit some teens from taking up the habit.

But it's those already addicted who are hardest to reach. It is evening now in Rye, New York, and Paul is standing on the lawn outside the rec hall, where he has just played acoustic guitar with his band. "Yeah, I sucked tonight," he says, smoking a cigarette with two friends. The group is asked if higher cigarette prices make a difference to them. "Not really," says Emily, a pack-a-day 17-year-old who lost her grandfather to lung cancer. "It just means that if I have to make a choice between spending my money on cigarettes or food, I'll skip the food." Paul confessed he'd take the cash from his parents' wallets for cigarettes, sticking to singles so they wouldn't notice.

The good news is that to some extent, almost every kid I spoke to is already halfway there: They all say they plan on quitting eventually.

"I definitely don't plan on being one of those yucky mommies you see rolling their kid in a stroller while they're sucking on some nasty cigarette," says Kristin, the Seattle high school student. "I mean, I know I'm going to stop."

Has she ever tried seriously to quit? "Oh, yeah," she says. And was she successful? She rolls her eyes as only a teenager can, though it's unclear who, or what, is annoying her. "No," she says finally. "I guess I wasn't."

2

Teen Smoking Is a Serious Problem

Bruce Epstein

Bruce Epstein practiced pediatrics in St. Petersburg, Florida, for twenty-six years. He is the editor of the website www.kidsgrowth.com.

Many teenagers begin smoking because they underestimate the likelihood that they will become addicted to cigarettes. In the United States, however, 6 million teens continue to smoke, despite their knowledge of potential health hazards, and studies show that 75 percent of teens who begin smoking in high school are still smoking five years later. Nicotine is a "gateway" drug, which means that teens who smoke are more likely to go on to use other drugs, such as alcohol, marijuana, and cocaine, than teens who do not smoke. Teens who smoke may feel they are immune to the negative health effects of smoking, but in fact they have more respiratory illnesses and more evidence of reduced lung growth than their nonsmoking peers.

True or false:

1. About 1,000 youngsters will smoke their first cigarette today.
2. Tobacco use can lead to illegal drug use in teens.
3. Most kids believe that smoking one cigarette will not hurt them.
4. Most teens who smoke feel that they can quit any time they choose.
5. Kids who smoke do not light up until they are well into high school.
6. Smokeless tobacco is not a problem for today's youth.
7. Cigarettes and smoking cause more deaths than AIDS, alcohol, car accidents, murders, suicides, illegal drugs and fires combined.
8. Adolescent girls who smoke and take oral birth control pills greatly increase their chances of having blood clots and strokes.
9. It is the "cool kids" who smoke.
10. The age at which smokers start to smoke has no effect on their ability to quit later.
11. Kids get their cigarettes mostly from vending machines, convenience stores and promotional give-aways.

12. Youthful cigarette smokers experience health problems only when they are older.

13. Most teens gain weight if they are able to quit smoking.

14. If your child's best friends smoke, your child's risk of taking up smoking is two times higher than if your child's best friends did not smoke.

The answers

1. False. Each day, 3,000 children smoke their first cigarette; that's more than 1-million annually. At least 3-million adolescents are smokers. Tobacco use primarily begins in early adolescence, typically by age 16; almost all first use occurs before high school graduation. Twenty percent of American teens smoke; roughly 6-million teens in the United States today smoke despite the knowledge that it is addictive and leads to disease.

2. True. For many teenagers, nicotine is a "gateway" drug involved in the development of other drug dependencies. Nicotine is a drug, make no mistake about it, and once the habit of giving drugs to oneself is established, beginning to use any other drug is often an easier decision. According to a recent report from the Office of the Surgeon General, teenagers who smoke were three times more likely to use alcohol, eight times more likely to smoke marijuana, and 22 times more likely to use cocaine than adolescents who did not smoke. In addition, tobacco use in adolescence is associated with other negative behavior, including fighting, carrying weapons and engaging in high-risk sexual behavior.

Of every 100,000 15-year-old smokers, tobacco will prematurely kill at least 20,000 before the age of 70.

---

3. True. Though the statement is true, the conclusion is false. Youngsters who smoke their first cigarette might immediately become short of breath, begin to cough, and experience nausea and dizziness. These symptoms can last as long as a week after smoking just one cigarette.

4. True. Children underestimate the likelihood that they will become addicted to tobacco. Although only 5 percent of high school smokers said that they would definitely be smoking five years later, close to 75 percent were still smoking 7 to 9 years later. The same survey found that about two-thirds of the adolescents who smoked said they wanted to quit, and 70 percent said they would not start smoking if they could make that choice again. Our current state of research suggests that nicotine is much more addictive than some drugs we consider very dangerous.

5. False. Research has shown that more than 21 percent of eighth-graders have used cigarettes, and more than 4 percent of eighth-graders report smoking half a pack of cigarettes or more each day. . . . So if you wait until your child reaches middle school to begin a discussion about tobacco use, it may already be too late.

6. False. A survey in 1998 revealed that more than 25 percent of boys between the ages of 12 and 17 had tried smokeless tobacco, an increase of more than 300 percent from a similar survey taken in 1988. More than

1-million adolescent boys use smokeless tobacco.

7. True. Tobacco-related illnesses kill more than 400,000 Americans each year. Of the 3,000 teens who started smoking today, nearly 1,000 will eventually die as a result of their smoking. Of every 100,000 15-year-old smokers, tobacco will prematurely kill at least 20,000 before age 70. More than 1,200 die each day in the United States because they smoked cigarettes. That is the same number of people who would be killed if four 747s crashed every day, killing all on board. Our government would take quick action to ground all 747s until the problem was fixed, yet we do little to stop people from killing themselves with tobacco—and the real tragedy is that almost 100 percent of people who smoke today started when they were still living with their parents.

8. True. If your daughter is using oral contraceptives and is smoking, you owe it to her to educate her about the risk of mixing the two.

9. False. Kids who smoke have lower self-images. The same is true for smokeless tobacco. Daily use of tobacco is highest among school dropouts. The Surgeon General's Report found that students with the highest grades are less likely to smoke than those with the lowest grades. About 7 percent of A-average students in high school are daily smokers, whereas nearly 50 percent of D-average students are daily smokers. Most athletes know that cigarette smoke will reduce their performance on the playing field.

10. False. A person who starts smoking at age 13 will have a more difficult time quitting, has more health-related problems and probably will die earlier than a person who begins to smoke at age 21. Alarming as it may sound, the fastest-growing segments of the population beginning to smoke are pre- and early teens. In fact, during the past few years, they are the only segment of the population whose rate of smoking has continued to climb.

11. True. Despite state laws prohibiting the sale of tobacco to minors, children can easily buy these products. One study found that, on average, children and adolescents were able to successfully buy cigarette products 67 percent of the time from convenience stores. Vending machines are a primary source of tobacco for young smokers. A study by the vending machine industry found that 22 percent of 13-year-old smokers use vending machines to get their cigarettes.

12. False. Kids who smoke experience changes in the lungs and reduced lung growth, and they risk not achieving normal lung function as an adult. Kids who smoke have significant health problems, including cough and phlegm production, decreased physical fitness and an unfavorable lipid profile. Kids who don't smoke have fewer respiratory illnesses.

13. False. Two-thirds of adolescents who quit smoking stay the same weight or even lose some.

14. False. If your child's best friends smoke, then your youngster is 13 times (yes, 13 times) more likely to smoke than if his or her friends did not smoke. This clearly demonstrates the importance of peer pressure in creating the atmosphere that leads to smoking.

3

Antismoking Efforts Should Target Both Adults and Teens

Mike A. Males

Mike A. Males serves on the California Wellness Foundation Adolescent Health Advisory Board, and he has written extensively on youth and social issues for the New York Times, *the* Lancet, Phi Delta Kappan, In These Times, *and* Scribner's Encyclopedia of Violence in America.

Antismoking groups' decision to focus only on preventing teenage smoking overlooks the problem that the large number of adult smokers make smoking seem socially acceptable to teens. Since smoking is more a conformist act than a rebellious one, antismoking groups and the tobacco industry make smoking more alluring through their "everybody does it" messages. Treating tobacco as a gateway drug (a substance that will cause teens to try other, harder drugs) is also doing more harm than good in the war against teen smoking. The gateway theory leads to the criminalization of teen smoking by restricting youth access to cigarettes and punishing teens who are caught smoking. If teens cannot get cigarettes in stores, however, they will find other means of access to them. Criminalizing smoking for teens is ineffective when smoking is otherwise deemed socially acceptable by adults. Thus the prevention of teen and adult smoking must be addressed together to change society's acceptance of smoking overall.

Politically-driven 1990s policy addresses social and health problems in simplistic, fragmented, good-versus-evil fashion whose concepts can be reduced to sloganeering. Youths and adults, however, experience whole environments, not the isolated segments this or that reform movement finds profitable to publicize in media-honed snippets and tinker with by legislated fiat. The influences of the whole environment must be considered if effective policy is to develop.

Reflecting the more integrated view of European public health strate-

Mike A. Males, *Smoked: Why Joe Camel Is Still Smiling.* Monroe, ME: Common Courage Press, 1999.

gies, the international medical journal *The Lancet* editorialized that "if governments really want to kick the public's smoking habit, they must begin to tackle adult tobacco consumption" rather than indulging the "cosmetic act" of just "kicking the teenage habit." The logic of anti-tobacco activists who attacked the editorial and defended [former President Bill] Clinton's politically-driven focus on youths failed to recognize that American health policies have scant record of shining success. A dissenter, Elizabeth Whelan of the American Council on Science and Health, agreed the policy was "more symbolism than substance."

The tobacco industry, whose survival depends upon its ability to understand the particular environmental elements that make smoking popular or unpopular, has won this battle hands down. Anti-smoking policy has been diverted in ineffectual, often silly, crusades against "youth access" to tobacco, the color and format of advertising icons, and campaigns ridiculing teenagers. (In California, for example, health department anti-smoking ads routinely disparaged youths for making tobacco moguls rich.) While satisfying to grownups (especially those in an official capacity who could be doing more themselves), these approaches have little to do with preventing smoking; some might actually reinforce it.

Despite the depiction of smoking as rebellious, it is actually conformist behavior.

In reality, high-risk teens and adults are heavily concentrated in the same families and communities. In 1997, smoking rates were more than twice as high among adults with a high school education or less than among college graduates. Thus, the first catastrophic mistake made by anti-tobacco forces—one caused by the injection of politicians' needs into health strategy—was to depict teenage smoking as reckless, rebellious behavior. This misportrayal flowed from the strategies employed by traditional anti-drug politicking, which seeks to create a good-evil "us-versus-them" scenario by connecting the targeted drug with a feared, disliked, powerless out-group. Such tactics have included linking marijuana to Latinos and cocaine to black musicians. Today, drugs and smoking are linked to young people.

Despite the depiction of smoking as rebellious, it is actually *conformist* behavior. Teenagers who smoke are seeking to be like adults around them who smoke, and cigarette use is seen in many families and communities as a marker of adulthood. As Glantz pointed out, the industry is well aware of the adult-teen connection in smoking and has tailored its promotion to take advantage of it. Unfortunately, by allowing political judgments to interfere with health strategy, anti-smoking lobbies have denied the fact that teen smokers are heavily influenced by adult smokers and have instead adopted strategies which reinforce the industry's efforts to profit from the connection. Ads by the Campaign for Tobacco-Free Kids nowhere mention parental influences. Breaking with [C. Everett] Koopera Surgeon General's reports, the 1994 report by Surgeon General Joycelyn Elders ignored both the precedence of parental influences and its own well-buried research findings. Parents can continue puffing, it said, so long as they moralize to their kids between drags:

> Parental tobacco use does not appear to be as compelling a
> risk [for teen smoking] as peer use; on the other hand, par-
> ents may exert a positive influence by disapproving of smok-
> ing, being involved in children's free time, discussing health
> matters with children . . .

Contrary to the Surgeon General's claim, the major study on that subject
showed children of smoking parents who disapproved of smoking were
more likely to smoke than children of nonsmoking parents who were in-
different.

As the Bogalusa Heart Study (discussed later) found, "adolescents rarely
expected their friends to favor, much less pressure them to begin, cigarette
smoking." In fact, kids' previous values and habits, strongly shaped by
home life, influence who they choose for peers, [the] authors pointed out.
"Researchers have consistently shown that similarity stems primarily not
from processes of peer influence but from adolescents' inclinations to
choose like-minded peers as friends and the tendency of peer groups to re-
cruit as new members individuals who already share the group's normative
attitudes and behaviors."

After denying adult influences, health groups have ridiculed teenagers as fools and dupes who must be subjected to severe punishments in
order to protect them from their own recklessness, which in turn is fos-
tered by innate teenage mental flaws, susceptibility to bad influences, and
pressuring peers. Because of developmental factors, "adolescents are thus
vulnerable to a range of hazardous behaviors and activities," Elders' report declared, ignoring a massive array of evidence that 1990s youth are
less vulnerable to behavior risks than are adults. The 1998 report by J.P.
Pierce and colleagues blames smoking on adolescent irrationality driven
by tobacco ads.

---

*[The] gateway theory holds that the merest deviance
from absolute virtue cannot be tolerated in young
people.*

Thus, the anti-smoking lobby insults its target group at the same time
it seeks to persuade it. Demeaning adolescents may be physically satisfying to grownups (and to those teenagers who identify with grownups), but
it is ill-founded and self-defeating. It is also misguided. Contrary to popular prejudices, large-scale research reviews reveal no evidence that adolescents harbor any less ability to appreciate long-term risks than adults do,
and the assumption that any disapproved behavior by a teenager portends
long-term disaster is an impediment to reasoned policy.

As with the "adult" nature of smoking, the tobacco industry gleefully
echoed this official theme as well. "Powerful pressure from their peers,"
R.J. Reynolds Tobacco Company declared in a full-page ad in 1995, ". . .
is one of the most influential factors in a child's decision to smoke." Thus,
"parents," the tobacco giant declared, shoulder to shoulder with Clinton's Surgeon General, must "add [their] voice to the many others trying

to discourage kids from smoking . . . Listen. Empathize. Be involved . . . you might begin reminding your child that studies have identified smoking as a risk factor for certain diseases." The industry did not go so far as to urge parents to discourage their kids from smoking and to avoid these diseases by quitting smoking themselves! Nor did the president or Surgeon General.

Teenagers, health lobbies and the industry chorused in unison, are immature children too unsophisticated to practice an "adult" habit like smoking. Sadly, kids, pressured by their foolish peers, light up anyway in defiance of the healthy advice of government officials and the tobacco industry.

"Everybody does it"

Yet another key common ground between supposed anti- and pro-tobacco forces exists when they depict smoking as common to teenhood. Given the politically-driven assumptions underlying them, it's no surprise that the array of "anti-smoking" strategies designed around the assumption that teenagers are reckless and rebellious—that is, strategies in denial of the adult-teen smoking link—have been truly stupid.

"Meet the Philip Morris Generation," announced a Campaign for Tobacco-Free Kids advertisement, one of three dozen ads posted on its website (www.tobaccofreekids.org, June 1999). "Five Million Kids Smoke," blared another, referring to the number of 12–17 year-olds who tried at least one cigarette in the previous month—nowhere mentioning that "20 Million Kids Don't Smoke." This latter point would not be merely rhetorical, but crucial, given the Surgeon General's claim that the main reason kids smoke is peer pressure. None of these ads mentioned that teenagers smoke because adults (particularly parents) smoke, or that older family members are usually kids' first source of cigarettes. . . . The Campaign's ads depicted teens as mere dupes of tobacco marketing.

Thus, anti-smoking groups, in a tactic that is both false and self-defeating, portray smoking as sweeping the teenage population, a normative behavior for adolescents. "Almost one-quarter of all adults are current smokers, along with more than a third of all high school students," the Campaign for Tobacco-Free Kids declares on its 1999 website and national ad pitch for big tobacco-settlement bucks for "prevention."

This is a false comparison. It equates smoking once or more in the past *month* by high school *seniors* (not all students) with heavy *daily* smoking by adults (in which the heavier smoking rates among adults of parental age are diluted by combining them with lower smoking rates among persons over 65). The apples-apples comparison, one which would filter out experimental or occasional cigarette use, is daily, or heavier (half-pack-plus per day) smoking by high schoolers and adults of parental age. Here we find that about 30% of adults in the 25–64 range smoke daily, compared to about 22% of high school seniors (only 13% of high school seniors smoke half a pack per day or more, and younger students smoke even less). Parents are considerably more likely to smoke than their teen children are.

So, why would the anti-tobacco lobby exaggerate the prevalence of youth smoking? Exaggeration grabs favorable attention and makes it easier to raise money for anti-smoking interests. But the larger result of embellishment can be tragic. It reinforces the tobacco industry's message, particularly to youths in heavy-smoking communities, that cigarette use is a normal habit for teens to take up. As Glantz points out, "One reason that kids start to smoke is the fact that they grossly overestimate smoking prevalence. Ubiquitous tobacco advertising has contributed to this misimpression, but so has antitobacco education that says, 'resist your peers, don't smoke.' The message should be 'be like your friends, be a nonsmoker.'"

But this would mean affirming adolescents, and anti-smoking groups seem loath to do that. The heart of official anti-drug, and now 1990s antismoking, strategies is to tie the vilified habit to an unpopular group whose members, by definition, are "not like us" that is, fear of a drug is made synonymous with fear of the group, and vice-versa. To reverse field and affirm the fact that the large majority of adolescents don't smoke—that, in fact, adults smoke much more—would weaken this linkage.

"Gateway drugs": a good old-time religion

One of the tobacco industry's biggest allies is the lack of imagination, complemented by politically-driven stereotypes of young people, that infect anti-smoking thinking. Review of supposed big-picture analyses of adolescent behavior in the 1990s reveals the dismal conventionality of social and health science assumptions. Teens, they argue, are naturally reckless, corrupted by peers and pop culture, defying healthy grownups. That today's youth (the second generation exposed to modern drug risks) are avoiding hard drugs and substituting softer alternatives, a much less risky approach than displayed by baby-boom young adults (the first generation exposed to modern risks) 30 years ago, is a crucial point missed by many of today's health researchers.

Perhaps the most hallowed dogma of modern anti-drug and antismoking strategy is "gateway" theory. Gateway theory holds that if a youth reaches age 21 without smoking (or drinking or using drugs or doing anything sinful), he/she never will do these things. Gateway theory further holds that the first act of corruption (taking a puff of tobacco, or, in Pierce's recent studies, even thinking about doing so) opens the floodgates to the next sin (drinking beer), then to marijuana, then to shoplifting, school dropout, slutdom, crack, heroin, gun-toting, armed robbery, suicide and/or schoolyard slaughter. Reasoning backwards, then, gateway theory holds that the merest deviance from absolute virtue cannot be tolerated in young people. This thinking creates a wide-open license for abuse since the true "gateway"—the "original sin"—can never be determined. For every bad behavior (say, smoking), there was a gateway to that (say, using profanity), and a gateway to that (saying "swell"), and to that (hanging out at the pool hall in River City).

Therefore, gateway theory's logic continues, more and more vicious punishments to stop lesser and lesser strayings by more and more kids at younger and younger ages must be deployed. This is why programs based on gateway theories enjoy permanent, endless expansion potential and employ ever-rising tones of hysteria regardless of what is really going on. This is why declines in, and low levels of, addiction are scary to gateway theorists and must be buried by even wilder fear tactics, as I witnessed many a time in several years' work in drug/alcohol programs. This is why "zero tolerance" policies (the remedies gateway theory promotes) culminate in evermore blatant administrative idiocies such as kicking kids out of school for increasingly minor infractions that harm no one (bringing an apple corer, lemon drops, tiny plastic-gun keychain, or Midol to school, to cite a few infamous examples of what the feisty youth-rights journal *Freedom Voice* calls "stupid adult tricks").

As one UK study points out, gateway theory has proven useless for designing effective health programs. The reason is that it is founded in a pointless tautology. For the small fraction of individuals who become addicts, everything is a "gateway" to something worse; for the large majority who don't become addicted, nothing is. Gateway theory really boils down to a political convenience, exonerating grownup misbehaviors while declaring adolescence the disease that infects all of society with its pathologies.

Gateway theory is popular because it embodies a no-risk validation of Americans' vicarious puritanism. In effect, adult behaviors are exempted from scrutiny, since the gateway theory's deterministic model portrays adults simply as the inevitable products of whatever they did as adolescents. Thus, gateway concepts allow adults to demand absolutist behaviors from young people that grownups do not demand of themselves. Notice how rarely those who push "zero tolerance" policies for drug or tobacco or alcohol use apply those standards to themselves or to their own peer group.

Joseph Califano Jr., Secretary of Health, Education and Welfare under [former President Jimmy] Carter and now director of Columbia University's Center on Addiction and Substance Abuse, is representative of true believers in gateway theory. He argues that drug, drinking, and smoking problems would disappear if we could just stop all adolescents everywhere from ever using these substances (a dictum Califano, an admitted daily scotch drinker, does not apply to himself).

> *The extreme, out-of-proportion punishments provoke more mistrust and reaction against authority than against smoking.*

A big flaw in that logic is called "selection bias" by social scientists. In this case, it means that people who never smoked at age 10 differ considerably from people who never smoked at age 21. Nearly everyone is or was a nonsmoker at age 10, which means this group resembles the general population. However, compared to the general population, persons who reach age 21 having never smoked at all are very different. They tend to be richer, come from families and locales where smoking is rare, and live in places like Utah and California and not in Kentucky and North Carolina. The gateway crowd, fixated on worry that one small experimentation or misstep will automatically spell addiction and ruin, ignores these critical factors that determine how likely someone is to wind up smoking.

Absolute adolescent abstinence is not simply impossible to achieve for reasons of efficiency alone; it would not be desirable even if it could be achieved. Addiction and abuse are not qualities of young age, nor even of drug use, but of individuals and circumstances. It is true that most people who abuse drugs first used drugs in adolescence, but that is also true of most people who don't abuse drugs. Example: 77 million Americans have used illicit drugs, 177 million alcohol, and 152 million cigarettes, with nearly all trying the drug first in young years. However, 95% of present or former illicit drug users, 90% of all present and former drinkers, and 70% of all present and former cigarette users, are not addicts. If adolescence itself were the major risk for taking up smoking, we would not expect to see smoking rates among Kentucky teens four times higher than among Utah teens, let alone the even wider gaps when factors like income, gender, and smoking by family adults are added in. Constrained by popular politics, 1990s gateway theory does not venture near the true gateway to unhealthy adolescent behavior, which is the social acceptability of corresponding behavior.

Criminalizing teen smoking

Thus, another common salvo of modern policy, once again endorsed by both anti-smoking and tobacco interests, has squandered vast amounts of time and effort trying to forcibly prevent teenage "access" to tobacco. Both anti-smoking groups and the industry championed the "no sales to under 18" crusade with zeal, the former to reap good press from highly visible "sting" operations against stores, the latter to enhance the value of smoking in the eyes of teens. Because of the adult-teen smoking link, efforts to use criminal penalties to forcibly prevent children and youths from acquiring tobacco are pointless: "There is no consistent evidence of a substantial effect on prevalence or consumption of tobacco among kids," Glantz argues.

The centerpiece of the recent "landmark" Food and Drug Administration rules governing tobacco, requiring photo identification from buyers who appeared to be under age 27, is silly. If inconvenienced by laws, kids get their smokes from grownup habitués. A moment's thought would affirm that there is no feasible way to prevent teenagers from acquiring cigarettes. If, after vigorous and sustained policing (the kind only a few suburban forces have the spare time to accomplish), 100% of tobacco retailers miraculously cut off sales to persons under age 18 whose ages are perfectly ascertained through tamper-proof identification, then youths will simply obtain cigarettes from any one of the dozens of smoking adults around them.

This, of course, is the case with every other vice "forbidden" to youths, such as alcohol and guns. For a few examples of many, two-thirds of high school seniors who drink do so with adults age 30 and older (imagine how much higher the percentage would be if they were asked about drinking partners 21 and older!), and all of the youths who committed the highly-publicized school shootings in 1998 and 1999 obtained their firearms from "responsible adults" (mostly their parents or relatives). Given that it's legal for adults to have sex with youth as young as 16 in most states, and two-thirds of pregnancies among girls under 18 are caused by adults, imagine the impracticality (the ludicrousness, in fact) of attempting to enforce an edict against grownups providing their younger bed partners with a beer or a smoke.

Indeed, evaluations of these access laws show unfavorable results. A detailed study by Massachusetts General Hospital researchers in the *New England Journal of Medicine* in 1997 found that criminalizing youth smoking was associated with a large, statistically significant *increase* in teen smoking. Researchers compared 500 tobacco sales outlets and the smoking levels of 22,000 students in grades 9–12 in three Massachusetts cities which vigorously enforced laws against cigarette sales to persons under age 18 and three similar cities that undertook no enforcement. Strong enforcement of tobacco sales laws (eight compliance checks in two years, including warning letters to and $200 fines levied against retailers who sold tobacco to youths, in the three enforcement cities) did have a big impact on the retailers. More than 80% of the merchants in the high enforcement communities were induced to refuse to sell to youths. This was double the number in the three communities with no enforcement.

But the key issue here wasn't the behavior of the merchants, it was teen smoking. Among youths, smoking trends were more discouraging in the cities that strongly enforced the law than in those that let kids buy smokes without hassle. In fact, in the two years after the tough enforcement regime was implemented, daily smoking rose sharply among teens in the crackdown towns (up 23%) but stayed the same in the laid-back burgs (down 2%); trends for monthly smoking were similar (up 12% in the heavy-enforcement cities, no change in the no-enforcement cities). Interestingly, the rates of youths' experimenting with (trying once) cigarettes did not change much (down 1% in the heavy-enforcement and down 2% in the no-enforcement cities).

Taken together, these findings strongly indicate that the biggest effect of tough "no-sales-to-youth" enforcement was (a) to *increase* the percentage of teens who smoked and (b) to hasten the transition of youths from experimentation to regular, then daily smoking. The new Food and Drug Administration regulation banning tobacco sales to minors "cannot reasonably be expected to reduce the supply of tobacco to young people or alter their smoking behavior," the authors of the study concluded.

Not surprisingly, researchers also discovered that the Tobacco Institute's voluntary "It's the Law" program against retail sales to youths was equally useless. The industry was acting in its rational self-interest to embrace such "anti-smoking" policies, which clearly do not reduce smoking, and apparently even promote it. But in the face of such dramatically negative findings, the unswerving promotions of "youth access" prohibitions by health lobbies appear irrational or ill-motivated.

If get-tough doesn't work, get tougher

The final, and crowning policy disaster has been to attempt to severely punish teenagers for smoking while at the same time ignoring, or even justifying, adult smoking. Measures to expel from school, deny driver's licenses, require excessive fines and "community service," and even jail youths caught with cigarettes have been pushed by anti-smoking lobbies and enthusiastically endorsed by the industry. If criminalizing teens for smoking and penalizing them for doing so were key to creating a smoke-free society in the future, one might wonder why the tobacco-industry-dominated state of North Carolina imposes some of the most severe penalties for teen smoking. That a state which grows two-thirds of the nation's tobacco would enact tough laws against youth access shows just how small a threat such laws are to the industry.

Today's authorities have demonstrated that there is no limit to the restrictions or punishments that may be imposed for violations of vicarious puritanism—teenage coffee drinking, any kind of consumer spending, even the right to walk into stores without grownup supervision, now are coming under fire. When lawmakers and other officials impose arrests, fines, drivers' license suspensions, school expulsions, and jailings on teenagers who smoke, the extreme, out-of-proportion punishments provoke more mistrust and reaction against authority than against smoking. However, since few teens are caught smoking, it is probably not the punishing measures against teen smoking that caused the recent smoking increase so much as the irrelevance of those measures to the real forces influencing youth trends. When authorities ignore the serious conditions of life that rising numbers of teenagers confront, such as poverty, chaotic homes, and parents and adults debilitated by drugs, drinking, and drug-related crime, then young people react by ignoring an authority which has made itself irrelevant to their lives.

The extremism gateway logic leads to can be seen in the ideal now being pushed by major institutions and agencies such as the Carnegie Council on Adolescent Development and the Centers for Disease Control. Recent monitoring proposals from these and other institutes amount to round-the-clock surveillance of 30 million teenagers in order to deter the fraction of their number who might misbehave. Carnegie, for one example, has repeatedly pushed programs "to extend family- and school-like functions into the crucial after-school, summer, and weekend hours when neither schools nor parents are available to provide supervision." As agencies increasingly paint "out-of-school time" as the crucible of "substance abuse, sexual activity. . . and crime and violence," and as curfews and policing increasingly seek to remove youths from public space, programmatic monitoring, that at first appeared to stem from benign service goals, takes on an increasingly compulsory tone. Ironically, for increased supervision to prevent smoking, youths would have to be separated from their families, since, as the large-scale Bogalusa Heart Study reported in 1997, older relatives are the most common source of children's first cigarettes.

The larger trends accompanying the Clinton era's increasingly punitive anti-smoking policies also are clear. Teenage smoking had been declining for two decades before 1990s health policy decided to attack it. The result: after bottoming out at 17% in 1992, daily smoking by high school seniors rose to 22% in 1998. Half-pack-per-day or more smoking rose from 10% to 12.6%. Smoking at least once per month in 1998 had returned to its high levels of the 1970s. More recently, the smoking decline among young adults, then older adults, reversed and also started to rise.

And so, after nearly a decade of youth-obsessed policy emphasizing pyramiding restrictions, the newest studies, especially the 1999 Harvard college survey reported in *USA Today*, find "more students are lighting up than at any time in the past two decades, despite increasingly stringent attempts to stop them." Note: if the nation *abolished* controls on teenage smoking and a 28% increase occurred in six years, as the Harvard study claimed (or, if a town *legalized* teen cigarette smoking and a 23% increase in daily smoking ensued, as occurred after the New England crackdowns on tobacco sales to youths), the screams for a return to get-tough regimes would be deafening. Yet get-tough measures themselves seem immune to scrutiny despite their manifest failure. These abysmal results provoked no reevaluation of anti-smoking strategies.

Kids! You're too immature to smoke!

Because teenage smoking is heavily influenced by adult smoking, the two must be addressed together. So long as adults smoke in large numbers, teenagers around them will take up smoking. So long as teenagers take up smoking, a future of adult smokers is guaranteed. So long as government protects the social acceptability of adult smoking, reflected in permissive smoking policies, low prices, and the widespread marketing of tobacco products in hundreds of thousands of retail outlets, youths justifiably will view smoking as a reasonable choice, no matter what rhetorical "messages" health authorities send. The reason, as one UK study shows, is that youths who are most likely to smoke evaluate social practices based not on what grownups say, but on what they see grownups do. And so long as anti-smoking groups and the industry continue to tacitly agree on these policies, smoking will be a prominent feature of American life and death.

4

Laws to Prevent Youth Access to Cigarettes Are Ineffective

P.M. Ling, A. Landman, and S.A. Glantz

P.M. Ling, A. Landman, and S.A. Glantz are affiliated with the Center for Tobacco Control Research and Education, the Institute for Health Policy Studies, the Cardiovascular Research Institute, and the Center for AIDS Prevention Studies at the University of California, San Francisco.

Laws designed to prevent teens from acquiring cigarettes have failed to prevent teen smoking. In addition, focusing on such laws often has the effect of blaming teens, their friends, and their parents for teen smoking and may lead to more laws criminalizing teens for cigarette possession. The tobacco industry benefits from this approach to teen smoking prevention because it diverts attention away from its own marketing practices. Therefore, public health practitioners should abandon these ineffective preventative strategies by removing them from recommendations for comprehensive tobacco control policy. Instead, tobacco control advocates should pursue strategies with proven success rates. These include encouraging smoke-free workplaces and homes, raising taxes on cigarette sales, and increasing antismoking media campaigns and messages about the dangers of secondhand smoke.

The most widespread and popular strategy for reducing tobacco use has been "youth access" laws, which make it illegal to sell cigarettes to teenagers. In the USA, youth access controls have been part of tobacco control policies required by the federal government in order to obtain funding for substance abuse programmes; they were at the core of the tobacco regulation proposed by the Food and Drug Administration and struck down by the US Supreme Court. Both the US Centers for Disease Control and Prevention and the Institute of Medicine recommend youth access controls as part of a comprehensive tobacco control program. By August 2001, in the USA all 50 states and 1139 local governments had passed youth access laws.

Unfortunately, while these programmes do make it difficult for teens

P.M. Ling, A. Landman, and S.A. Glantz, "It Is Time to Abandon Youth Access Tobacco Programmes: Youth Access Has Benefited the Tobacco Industry," *Tobacco Control*, vol. 11, March 2002, p. 3. Copyright © 2002 by the British Medical Association. Reproduced by permission.

to purchase cigarettes, on the whole they do not affect teen smoking prevalence. Proponents of youth access programmes have argued that this approach would be effective, if only the programmes were "done right" and successfully prevented a high proportion of youth from using commercial sources to buy cigarettes, and that exceeding a high "threshold" level of merchant compliance is necessary to affect youth smoking. There is no consistent empirical evidence to support the existence of this hypothesised threshold.

A paper by S.E. Jones and colleagues explains why enforcement of youth access laws does not affect teen smoking. Using data from the Youth Risk Behavior Survey to describe the usual sources of cigarettes for high school student smokers, they found that in addition to purchasing cigarettes from stores, students give others money to buy cigarettes, borrow cigarettes from others, and sometimes steal them or use vending machines. From 1995 to 1999, significantly fewer student smokers purchased cigarettes. Consistent with earlier studies, they conclude that as youth access laws make it harder to purchase cigarettes, teens simply use other means to get cigarettes. They conclude, correctly, that the effectiveness of tobacco access laws are undermined by these other "social sources" of cigarettes. They recommend stricter enforcement of tobacco access laws and interventions to reduce social sources of cigarettes.

This recommendation is bad policy for four reasons. Firstly, there is no consistent evidence that increased enforcement of youth access laws affects youth smoking. These results are not surprising because, although most smokers start experimenting with cigarettes in their teens, few teens smoke daily. Indeed, the majority of teen smokers are "experimenters" who have smoked less than 100 cigarettes in their lifetime. It is virtually impossible to locate and target the few cigarettes needed to drive these irregular light smoking patterns. Secondly, trying to restrict "social sources" of cigarettes is impractical, blames children, their friends and parents, may lead to laws criminalising children for possession of cigarettes, and further diverts attention from tobacco industry marketing practices. Indeed, Philip Morris has embraced this tactic, and is actively promoting messages telling parents to keep their cigarettes away from their kids. Thirdly, this message is unlikely to resonate with teens, since one of the strongest perceived benefits of smoking is using cigarettes as a way to connect with others, particularly in the face of opposition. Fourthly, and most important, there is no evidence to suggest that trying to restrict social sources of cigarettes would work any better at reducing teen smoking prevalence than restricting commercial access.

It has been argued that even if they do not affect youth smoking prevalence, youth access programmes are valuable because they are politically safer than policies involving clean indoor air or anti-tobacco media campaigns, and that they engage the public and help build coalitions for tobacco control. While this may be true for tobacco control advocates, it is even more true for the tobacco industry.

Retailer training to fight tobacco control

Retailer training programmes focusing on youth access have facilitated tobacco industry development of a badly needed network at the local level to help defeat tobacco control efforts. This network has provided the industry with an extensive "early warning" network to identify emerging threats of the full range of tobacco control policies.

By 1992 the Tobacco Institute was using its "It's the Law" programme, which nominally trained retailers to ask purchasers for identification, alongside its efforts to urge retailers to monitor for local tobacco control efforts, including self service cigarette display bans and public smoking restrictions, so the Tobacco Institute could mobilise them to fight these tobacco control efforts: "For monitoring purposes, we [the Tobacco Institute] fund our allies in the convenience store groups to regularly report on ordinance introductions and assist in campaigns to stop unreasonable measures . . . Promotion of The Institute's "It's the Law" programme and other industry programmes play a helpful role as well."

Philip Morris took over the "It's the Law" programme in 1994. A 1994 speech by Ellen Merlo, senior vice president of corporate affairs at Philip Morris, details how alliances with local retailers allowed the industry to fight legislation: ". . . with . . . local activity rampant, we realized we had to have some way to control the bleeding. We needed an effective system to let us know when and where local laws were being proposed, either at town meetings, in the local city councils or by Boards of Health. Working with the New England Convenience Store Association and other tobacco companies, we developed a network whereby local retailers could assist us by providing information on legislative activities in every Massachusetts Community. We've discovered that if we have enough advance notice to do some homework and get somebody there for the public hearing, we can make a difference."

These programmes have helped the industry fight effective tobacco control legislation and educational programmes by creating the illusion that they are doing something.

The convenience stores also provide coverage for the industry to fight a wide range of effective tobacco control policies, including clean indoor air. For example, in Ohio, Philip Morris gained endorsements from the Ohio Grocers Association, the Ohio Association of Convenience Stores, the Ohio Petroleum Retailers and Repair Association, and the Ohio Petroleum Marketers Association for its "Ask First/It's the Law" programme. These organisations later provided Philip Morris cover for working to pass a law preempting the ability of local boards of health to enact smoke free workplace and restaurant regulations. When this legislation was proposed in the state legislature in 1995, the restrictions on local boards of health were hidden in what appeared to be primarily youth access legislation, entitled "The Comprehensive Smoking Regulation and Prevention of Youth Access to Tobacco Act of 1995". The Ohio Council of Retail Merchants, the Ohio Grocers Association, the Ohio Association of Convenience Stores, the Ohio Petroleum Retailers and Repair Association, and the Ohio Petroleum Marketers Association joined with restaurant, licensed beverage, and vending associations supporting this bill, while tobacco companies avoided mention. Philip Morris also drafted letters and phone scripts to contact individual retailers urging them to write their legislators to support this bill. The bill was defeated, but reappeared in 2001, when the primary public support for a bill restricting health boards' ability to make local smoking policies was the Ohio Council of Retail Merchants. The tobacco industry stayed out of the public eye, and politicians supporting Philip Morris' bill claimed they were simply supporting merchants.

Other benefits to the tobacco industry

Youth access programmes have also been widely supported by the tobacco industry, perhaps because they reinforce the industry's key marketing message that "smoking is for adults", which arguably makes smoking even more attractive to teens. The industry has widely publicised its own youth access programmes, such as "It's the Law", "We Card", and "Action Against Access". Some have argued that the industry programmes are "bad" in comparison with the "good" programmes run by health groups because they do not include vigorous enforcement efforts. To the general public, however, these programmes are indistinguishable.

These programmes have helped the industry fight effective tobacco control legislation and educational programmes by creating the illusion that they are doing something. They can also bolster industry credibility. Philip Morris has monitored the effect of their "Action Against Access" programme on smokers' awareness that Philip Morris started the programme, and how the programme affected consumers feelings about their company. Philip Morris's 1995 "Talking points to key customers on youth issue" emphasises how Philip Morris could benefit in the long term if it took the lead in addressing the sensitive "youth access" issue: "If we can frame proactive legislation or other kinds of actions on the Youth Access issue, if we can get out in front on this issue now, if we can seize the moral high ground, we will not only be doing the right thing, we will be protecting our industry for decades to come."

A 1991 Tobacco Institute discussion paper noted: "Broad-based advertising [of industry youth programmes] . . . has the important effect of making the public aware that the industry says it is trying to do the right thing. . . ."

The tobacco industry's vocal support of youth access programmes is similar to tobacco industry "accommodation" campaigns in response to pending clean indoor air laws. Accommodation campaigns aim to convince decision makers that legislation (such as smoke-free bars or restaurants) is unnecessary because establishments can take voluntary action to accommodate smokers and nonsmokers. The accommodation message allows the tobacco industry to take a political stance that appears reasonable: "we want to accommodate both smokers and non-smokers" and that makes health advocates appear extreme when advocating for clear indoor air. Similarly, youth access programmes allow the tobacco industry to appear to want to discourage youth smoking, thus seizing the "political centre" and "forcing health advocates to the extreme". In fact, the Tobacco Institute strategy planned to "bait anti-tobacco forces to criticize industry efforts" and "focus media on anti's extremism". The suggestions by Jones and colleagues and others to try to stop teens from obtaining cigarettes from their friends or parents will be even easier for the industry to paint as "extreme".

In addition to using youth access programmes to fight more effective policies, the tobacco industry has reaped several other benefits. Tobacco industry youth access messages (which do not contradict cigarette advertising) have allowed the industry to create competition with other media campaigns (such as the "Truth" campaign which exposes tobacco industry manipulation of teens) which actually affect teen smoking prevalence.

At best, youth access programmes are ineffective and a drain on limited resources. Even if they did affect youth smoking, the impact on smoking prevalence and morbidity and mortality from smoking would not be seen for decades. At worst, they are counterproductive and help the tobacco industry fight meaningful tobacco control policy. While youth access programmes seemed logical and well meaning, the simple fact is that they do not work and are now leading into even more futile efforts to control "social sources" of cigarettes.

It is time for public health practitioners to recognise that the balance of empirical evidence shows that youth access is a failed strategy and abandon it. Youth access should be removed from recommendations for comprehensive tobacco control programmes. Instead, tobacco control advocates should pursue strategies which have solid empirical evidence of effectiveness, such as smoke-free workplaces and homes, taxes, media campaigns, and secondhand smoke messages.

5

Antismoking Campaigns Make Smoking More Attractive to Teens

Mark Bowden

Mark Bowden is a writer for the Knight-Ridder/Tribune News Service.

According to a 2002 survey of teenagers, the multimillion-dollar antismoking campaign, "Think. Don't Smoke." actually encourages teens to smoke. Teens are commonly known to be drawn to activities they are told not to do. Many teens view cigarettes as having the added attraction of offering a sense of freedom and sexual maturity. Teens often admire the rebelliousness and defiance that is associated with smoking. The best way to curb teen smoking, then, is to stop making smoking attractive to teens by treating it as taboo.

A new survey of teenagers has shown that a multimillion-dollar anti-smoking campaign, the "Think. Don't Smoke" ads, actually encourages them to smoke cigarettes.

Well duh! I could have saved Philip Morris a lot of money, as could most parents of teenagers. I am not going to propose glib truisms here about teens. I have close relationships with two, and experience with their three older siblings. They are all different. But I don't think I'm being too bold here to point out that teens are prone to try everything, and they are especially drawn to the things they are told they should not.

The study, published in the American Journal of Public Health, questioned 9,000 young people between the ages of 12 and 17. The ads featured clean-cut-looking youths explaining why they don't smoke. Think back to when you were in high school. Now try to remember the most perfect, squeaky-clean kid you knew, the one who ran the student council, or who got the annual math department award. Now imagine that person on TV telling you, as a teen, not to do something.

To me, it comes as no surprise whatsoever that at the same time our country has become increasingly fanatical about not smoking, teen smoking remains a stubborn problem. The louder we inveigh against tobacco, the more attractive it becomes to young people. Substitute the word anything for the word tobacco in the previous sentence.

> *The louder we inveigh against tobacco, the more attractive it becomes to young people.*

One of my boys took up cigarettes for a while. It bothered me a lot, especially the realization that there was nothing I could do about it beyond insisting that it not happen in my house—and even that required vigilance, threats, and great displays of indignation. This was a kid whose mother wouldn't let him eat sugar for most of the first five years of his life, who was raised in a family of nonsmokers going back several generations. My late father had been a heavy smoker until the first Surgeon General's report linking tobacco to cancer came out in the early 1960s, at which point he stopped cold. He told me he craved a cigarette every day for almost 30 years afterward, until the day he died. Such was the familial conviction against the vice.

One day one of my neighbors, a good friend, told me he had encountered my son smoking at a local convenience store. The smoking part was by then not a surprise. But my friend found him leaning over a plastic container, pumping gasoline into it with a cigarette dangling from his lips. The neighbor said he ran across the lot and took the cigarette from my son's lips, and tried to explain the extreme hazards it posed (not just to him, but to everyone nearby).

The story, was illustrative. Certainly my son knew that a lit cigarette over a can of gasoline was dangerous, just as surely as he knew smoking was bad for his health. At some level I'm sure he even cared about those things. The point is that he wasn't thinking about those things at that moment. To a far greater extent than we adults, teenagers still possess the child's gift for living in the moment. So things like future plans and even potential bad consequences don't weigh strongly in their minds. They also tend to assume that nothing bad will ever happen to them, which is perfectly reasonable because, in most cases, nothing has.

Teens want to be cool

The best examination of the teen-smoking phenomenon I have seen is in [Malcolm] Gladwell's book "The Tipping Point." Citing a study by British psychologist Hans Eysenck, he sketches the characteristics of heavy smokers. They tend to be impulsive, risk-taking, have a higher-than-normal sex drive, and a tendency to be more rebellious and defiant. These are all, of course, attributes that teens admire. As Gladwell writes about smoking trend-setters: "They weren't cool because they smoked. They smoked because they were cool."

Teenagers are influenced by cool people, which rules out parents. And what to a teenager is cool? To be seen as adult, independent and brave. The cigarette advertises freedom and sexual maturity. It says, "I am a grown-up; nobody tells me what to do, and I'm not afraid."

I doubt that this is going to change any time soon.

This doesn't mean we shouldn't continue to educate people about tobacco's health risks. Education works—for adults. But the best way to curb teenage smoking is to stop making such a big deal about it.

The good news is that less than a third of those who try cigarettes in their youth continue smoking as they get older. My son abandoned the habit when he went away to college. My theory is that when he no longer had to listen to my rants, the habit lost its fun.

6

Countermarketing Campaigns Can Reduce Teen Smoking

Matthew C. Farrelly et al.

Matthew C. Farrelly is a researcher with Research Triangle Institute, an independent, nonprofit organization devoted to scientific research and technological development.

The American Legacy Foundation, a nonprofit antismoking organization, has created the "truth" campaign, which highlights alleged wrongdoings by the tobacco industry and works to counter tobacco marketing efforts. This campaign increases youths' antitobacco sentiments and reduces teen smoking. On the other hand, Philip Morris, a large tobacco company, produces the "Think. Don't Smoke." campaign, which takes focus away from the tobacco industry by simply offering youths directives not to smoke. These ads have a counterproductive effect on their teen audience. Youths exposed to the "Think. Don't Smoke." campaign ads actually report an increased openness to smoking. These results suggest that ads targeting the tobacco industry are more effective than messages that simply tell teens to say "no."

In early February 2000, the American Legacy Foundation (Legacy) launched "truth," a national tobacco countermarketing campaign conducted by an alliance of advertising firms led by Arnold Communications, Legacy staff, and nationwide youths. "Truth" targets primarily 12- to 17-year-olds who are susceptible to smoking. The core strategy of the campaign is to market its message as a brand, like other youth brands (e.g., Nike, Sprite), to appeal to youths most at risk of smoking. "Truth" TV and print commercials feature what advertising experts call "edgy" youths (i.e., those who are on the cutting edge of trends), promotional items (e.g., T-shirts, stickers), street marketing, and a Web site (www.thetruth.com). Although "truth" is a national multiethnic campaign, special components were developed to reinforce its appeal to African Americans, Hispanics, and Asians.

While drawing youths to "truth," the campaign delivers stark facts about tobacco and tobacco industry marketing practices, rather than sending directive "just say no" messages such as those used in the Philip Morris Company's "Think. Don't Smoke." campaign, which began in 1998. Specifically, many of the "truth" advertisements are based on historical statements from the industry itself that reveal its youth marketing and obfuscation of tobacco's health effects. In unmasking these practices, "truth" seeks to replace the attractive identity portrayed by tobacco advertising with a "truth" alternative identity.

The "truth" brand builds a positive, tobacco-free identity through hard-hitting advertisements that feature youths confronting the tobacco industry. This rebellious rejection of tobacco and tobacco advertising channels youths' need to assert their independence and individuality, while countering tobacco marketing efforts. For example, one well-known "truth" commercial, known as "Body Bags," features youths piling body bags outside of a tobacco company's headquarters and broadcasting loudly via megaphones that these represent the 1200 people killed daily by tobacco.

> *This rebellious rejection of tobacco and tobacco advertising channels youths' need to assert their independence and individuality, while countering tobacco marketing efforts.*

Empirical evidence for the potential benefits of the national "truth" campaign's approach comes from the dramatic decline in youth tobacco use associated with the Florida and Massachusetts campaigns, as well as from other studies that have found campaigns focusing on tobacco industry practices to be effective.

Legacy's model is that "truth" will change youths' attitudes toward smoking, and that this in turn will change their smoking behavior, prevent them from initiating smoking, or both. Thus, attitude shifts are all intermediate outcome on the path to changing smoking behavior. A telephone survey of youths in Florida and nationwide demonstrated that attitudes toward tobacco changed dramatically among Florida youths compared with youths in the rest of the United States after the first year (1998) of Florida's "truth" campaign, compared with a national sample of youths whose attitudes remained relatively constant. The accompanying change in smoking prevalence was at first statistically nonsignificant, but results from the Florida Youth Tobacco Survey showed drops in smoking among middle-school and high-school students of 18% and 8%, respectively, after year 1 and of 40% and 18% after year 2.

Some assert that a portion of this decline can be attributed to the November 1998 $0.45-per-pack price increase. Cigarette prices increased by roughly 30% during 1998, year 1 of the Florida program, and by 7% during year 2. With price increases of this magnitude, economic studies projected a 10% to 20% decline in youth smoking prevalence for 1998 and a 2% to 5% decline for 1999. This suggests that although a significant fraction of the decline in smoking after the first year of Florida's program may have been due to price increases, the price increases alone cannot account for all of the 1998 decline or for the confined decline in smoking in 1999.

In the present study, we used the results of 2 national youth surveys to compare exposures to Legacy's "truth" and Philip Morris's "Think. Don't Smoke." campaigns. We then analyzed changes in youths' attitudes, beliefs, and intentions regarding the tobacco industry and tobacco use 10 months into the "truth" campaign as a function of levels of exposure to each campaign.

"Truth" vs. "Think. Don't Smoke."

To monitor the impact of the "truth" campaign on attitudes and behavior, in 1999 Legacy began sponsoring the Legacy Media Tracking Surveys (LMTSs), which were designed to yield nationally representative samples of youths aged 12 to 17 and of young adults aged 18 to 24. We limited our analysis to 12- to 17-year-olds, the target audience for "truth." These 2-stage stratified-design surveys measured exposure to environmental tobacco smoke, access to tobacco products, knowledge and attitudes about tobacco, awareness of pro- and anti-tobacco advertising, and self-reported tobacco use and intentions. Before the "truth" campaign was launched (on February 7, 2000), the baseline telephone survey (LMTS-I) was conducted between December 6, 1999, and February 6, 2000. The next telephone survey (LMTS-II) was conducted between September 8, 2000, and December 23, 2000. . . .

Tobacco attitudes, beliefs, and counteradvertising exposure

The LMTS asked youths how strongly they agreed or disagreed (on a 5-point scale) with a series of attitude, belief, and behavioral-intent statements about the tobacco industry, youths' perceptions of tobacco's social acceptability, and youths' intentions to smoke during the next year. Nonsmokers were asked to report their likelihood of smoking any time in the next year. To show how these attitudes, beliefs, and intentions changed between the baseline and the follow-up surveys, we report the percentage . . . of 12- to 17-year-olds who agreed or strongly agreed with the targeted attitudes.

The LMTS contained questions to measure awareness of television advertisements from "truth" and "Think. Don't Smoke." First, respondents were asked in an open-ended question to report any antismoking or anti-tobacco campaigns of which they were aware. This measure of unaided recall allows us to track which campaigns are most prominent in the minds of youths over time. We then queried youths about their awareness of specific campaign advertisements by asking them whether they had "recently seen an anti-smoking or anti-tobacco ad on TV that———," followed by a brief description of the beginning of the advertisement. Questions were crafted to provide respondents with enough information to recognize the advertisement in question but not enough for them to "fake" awareness of it. A respondent who indicated recognition was then asked to report further ad details to confirm awareness. Confirmed awareness of 1 or more advertisements indicated campaign awareness or exposure. . . .

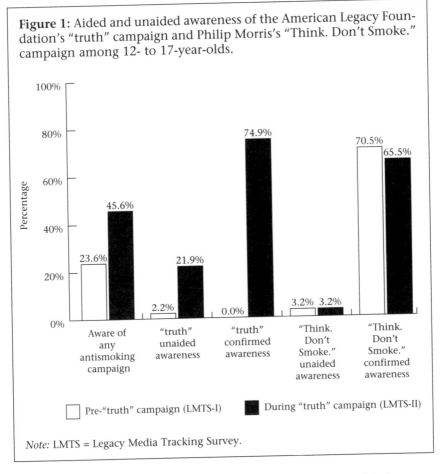

Figure 1: Aided and unaided awareness of the American Legacy Foundation's "truth" campaign and Philip Morris's "Think. Don't Smoke." campaign among 12- to 17-year-olds.

Note: LMTS = Legacy Media Tracking Survey.

We combined the 2 LMTSs . . . to elucidate the relationship between shifts in attitudes and beliefs and exposure to the "truth" and "Think. Don't Smoke." campaigns. The attitudes and beliefs in the LMTS address tobacco industry behavior, the social acceptability of tobacco use, and intentions to smoke during the next year. . . .

Changes in exposure to tobacco countermarketing campaigns

The percentage of 12- to 17-year-olds who reported awareness of any tobacco countermarketing campaign (Figure 1) doubled during the first 10 months of the "truth" campaign—from 23.6% to 45.6%. Awareness of the "truth" campaign accounted for much of this increase. With no prompting (unaided awareness), 22% of 12- to 17-year-olds in the LMTS-II indicated that they were aware of the "truth" campaign, compared with 3% who indicated awareness of "Think. Don't Smoke." Confirmed awareness of specific campaign advertisements among 12- to 17-year-olds was

Table 1: Percentages of 12- to 17-Year-Olds Who Agreed with Indicated Attitudes at Baseline and 10-Month Surveys

Attitude	LMTS-I (95%CI)	LMTS-II (95% CI)	% Change
Cigarette companies try to get young people to start smoking.	74.0 (71.3, 76.7)	83.0 (81.4, 84.6)	12.2
Cigarette companies lie.	74.7 (72.0, 77.3)	83.8 (82.2, 85.4)	12.3
Cigarette companies deny that cigarettes cause cancer and other harmful diseases.	48.4 (45.3, 51.5)	58.6 (56.4, 60.8)	21.0
Cigarette companies deny that cigarettes are addictive.	57.9 (54.8, 60.9)	64.0 (61.8, 66.1)	10.6
I would like to see cigarette companies go out of business.	70.4 (67.6, 73.2)	78.9 (77.0, 80.7)	12.0
I want to be involved in efforts to get rid of smoking.	65.2 (62.2, 68.1)	82.4 (80.7, 84.2)	26.4
Taking a stand against smoking is important to me.	72.1 (69.4, 74.9)	83.2 (81.4, 85.0)	15.4
Not smoking is a way to express your independence.	57.4 (45.9, 52.1)	70.1 (53.8, 58.6)	22.2
Smoking cigarettes makes people your age look cool or fit in.[a]	86.4 (84.2, 88.6)	92.1 (90.9, 93.3)	6.6
Do you think you will smoke a cigarette at any time during the next year?[b]	94.3 (92.8, 95.9)	95.9 (95.0, 96.8)	1.6

Note: LMTS = Legacy Media Tracking Survey; CI = confidence internal.
[a]Disagreed or strongly disagreed.
[b]Definitely not or probably not.

75% for "truth" and 66% for "Think Don't Smoke." The distribution of exposure to 1, 2, 3, and 4 or more advertisements was 23%, 19%, 14%, and 19% for "truth" and 37%, 21%, 6%, and 1% for "Think. Don't Smoke." in the LMTS-II.

Attitudes and beliefs about tobacco and intentions to smoke

Between surveys, the percentage of 12- to 17-year-olds who agreed with several attitudes and beliefs that are central to the "truth" campaign changed by an amount that ranged from 6.6% to 26.4% (Table 1). These attitudes and beliefs center on tobacco industry behavior (e.g., denying the health effects and addictive nature of tobacco), attitudes toward the tobacco industry (e.g., "should go out of business"), social acceptability of tobacco use (e.g., "not smoking is a way to express your independence" and "smoking makes you look cool"), and intention to smoke during the next year. The prevalence of youths who agreed (or disagreed if that was the target direction of attitudinal change) increased for all of these statements. The percentage of current nonsmokers who said that they probably or definitely would not smoke 1 year from the time of the survey also increased, but the change was not statistically significant. . . . Exposure to "truth" was associated with youths' attitudes toward the tobacco industry's marketing practices, its efforts to conceal tobacco's harmful effects, and the industry as a whole; for example, youths exposed to "truth" were more likely to agree that "cigarette companies try to get young people to start smoking.". . . Furthermore, a significant dose-response effect was seen with increased exposure to "truth." There was no association between this belief and either measure of exposure for "Think. Don't Smoke."

Exposure to "truth" was associated with a doubling of the odds that youths would agree that "cigarette companies lie," and increases in exposure to additional advertisements were associated with concomitant increases in the odds of agreeing with this statement. Exposure to "Think. Don't Smoke." advertisements showed no such associations. Although neither campaign influenced the percentage of youths who were aware of cigarette companies' past efforts to conceal tobacco's addictive properties, exposure to "truth" increased youths' awareness of how the industry concealed tobacco's deleterious health effects whereas exposure to "Think. Don't Smoke." had the opposite effect.

In contrast, the odds of agreeing that cigarette companies have denied that cigarettes cause disease declined by 24% with exposure to any "Think. Don't Smoke." advertisement and exposure to additional advertisements reinforced this effect. . . .

We constructed 4 models of youths' intentions and attitudes toward smoking. The first model examined youths' endorsement of the statement "I want to get involved in efforts to get rid of smoking" and the second examined their agreement that "taking a stand against smoking [was] important" to them. Exposure to the "truth" campaign was associated with a 35% and a 163% increase, respectively, in the odds of agreement with either of these statements. In addition, the more "truth" advertisements seen, the greater the odds of wanting to take a stand against smoking. Exposure to "Think. Don't Smoke." advertisements did not influence youths' level of agreement with either of these statements.

22% of 12- to 17-year-olds . . . indicated that they were aware of the "truth" campaign, compared with 3% who indicated awareness of "Think. Don't Smoke."

In the 2 other models, youths were asked whether they agreed that "not smoking is a way to express independence" and disagreed with the assertion that smoking makes youths "look cool or fit in." The odds ratios for "truth" campaign exposure were 1.46 and 1.52, respectively. The results for "Think. Don't Smoke." were similar, but the result for "looking cool" was only marginally statistically significant. . . .

Exposure to "truth" was associated with a marginally statistically significant decrease in the odds of current nonsmokers' expressing an intention to smoke any time in the next year, however, the dose-response relationship was not statistically significant. In contrast, exposure to "Think.

Don't Smoke." was associated with an increase in the odds of youths' intending to smoke in the next year, and the dose-response relationship was statistically more robust. . . .

The "truth" campaign changes teens' views of tobacco

Results from the 2 nationally representative surveys demonstrate that 10 months into the "truth" campaign, tobacco was more prominent in the minds of youths. Unaided awareness of tobacco countermarketing campaigns has nearly doubled. The "truth" campaign resonates more with youths than "Think. Don't Smoke," even though the "Think. Don't Smoke." campaign began in 1998 and aired for more than 12 months before the initial 10-month run of the "truth" campaign reported here.

"Think. Don't Smoke." was associated with an increase in the odds of youths' intending to smoke in the next year.

Exposure to the "truth" campaign also appears to have changed the way youths think about tobacco. The percentage of youths who held anti-tobacco attitudes and beliefs increased by an amount that ranged from 6.6% to 26.4% during the first 10 months of the campaign, which compares favorably with the 10% average increase in Florida during the first year of the campaign. Our results parallel the experience of Florida's "truth" campaign, in which strong shifts in attitudes preceded changes in behavior, despite a somewhat lower level of campaign awareness than was achieved in Florida.

The attitudes that changed most dramatically were "taking a stand against smoking is important," "not smoking is a way to express independence," and "cigarette companies deny that cigarettes cause cancer and other harmful diseases." These concepts are central to the strategy of "truth" and underlie advertisements such as "Body Bags," which featured teens challenging the tobacco industry by dragging body bags in front of a cigarette company's offices to remind them that they market a product that kills. These attitudinal changes were shown to be associated with youths' exposure to the "truth" campaign.

We believe that Philip Morris's "Think. Don't Smoke." campaign is clearly designed not to draw attention to tobacco industry marketing tactics or behavior; thus, the attitudes that relate to the tobacco industry do not represent a test of the success of its campaign. Interestingly, however, we found that exposure to "Think. Don't Smoke." engendered more favorable feelings toward the tobacco industry than we found among those not exposed to "Think. Don't Smoke." advertisements. This discovery lends support to the assertion of tobacco control activists that the purpose of the Philip Morris campaign is to buy respectability and not to prevent youth smoking. In addition, the campaign slogans "Think. Don't Smoke." (Philip Morris) and "Tobacco Is Whacko, if You Are a Teen" (Lorillard) are distinctly counter to recommendations made by the Columbia Expert Panel on youth tobacco countermarketing. This panel advises against directive messages such as those telling youths not to smoke and that smoking is uncool and for adults only.

Although the way in which exposure to "Think. Don't Smoke." affects young people's attitudes toward the tobacco industry may not be an appropriate measure by which to judge the performance of the campaign, the attitudes toward smoking included in our analyses are relevant to "Think. Don't Smoke." Our analyses indicate that although the level of confirmed awareness for both campaigns is roughly equal, "truth" has had a more consistent impact on attitudes toward smoking. Our quantitative analysis supports the findings of a focus-group study of 120 12- to 16-year-olds in Arizona, California, and Massachusetts. This study indicated that "Think. Don't Smoke." advertisements were the least effective among a group of advertisements including 10 representing several state campaigns. Youths rated advertisements that graphically, dramatically, and emotionally portrayed the serious consequences of smoking highest in terms of making them "stop and think about not using tobacco.". . .

In summary, our findings suggest that an aggressive national tobacco countermarketing campaign can have a dramatic influence within a short period of time on attitudes toward tobacco and the tobacco industry. These attitudinal changes were also associated with reduced intentions to smoke among those at risk. If these changes in attitude are predictive of future changes in tobacco use, as demonstrated in Florida, they indicate that the "truth" campaign is on its way to curbing tobacco use among youths.

7

State Antismoking Programs Work

National Cancer Policy Board, Institute of Medicine, and National Research Council

The National Cancer Policy Board, Institute of Medicine, and National Research Council are affiliated with the National Academy of Sciences, a private, nonprofit academy of scholars dedicated to the advancement of science and technology.

State tobacco control programs are an effective means of reducing smoking among people of all ages. The more multifaceted these programs are, the greater their levels of success and the more lives saved in the process. Some state-run antismoking initiatives that have proven especially effective include aggressive counteradvertising and education programs, smoke-free worksite policies, tax increases on tobacco products, and support of tobacco treatment programs. Youth access laws that prevent the sale of tobacco products to youths, however, are in need of greater merchant compliance before they can be deemed successful. All existing tobacco control programs should be evaluated often to ensure they are meeting and improving stated goals.

G rowing attention is focused on how states can prevent deaths due to tobacco use. Thus state governors, state legislators, and their staffs currently must decide whether to fund tobacco control programs, and, if they do, how much to spend on them.

The National Cancer Policy Board (a joint program of the Institute of Medicine and the National Research Council) is charged with carrying out policy analyses to help the nation deal with cancer; in 1997, it quickly identified tobacco's role as the foremost cause of cancer deaths as its first topic of concern. The board followed debates taking place in state capitals throughout 1998 and 1999, and decided in July 1999, in consultation with the Board on Health Promotion and Disease Prevention of the Institute of Medicine, that it would be useful to summarize evidence about the effectiveness of state tobacco control programs and to briefly describe those programs for state government officials.

Tobacco control will likely remain on the agenda of many states for several years. Public health advocates, tobacco firms, tobacco growers, retailers, and the general public have all been drawn into the debate. This report does not address the merit of tobacco control compared to alternative uses of state funds or attempt to balance the interests of contending stakeholders; instead, it focuses on the narrower question of whether state tobacco control programs can reduce smoking and save lives. As states contemplate increasing their tobacco control efforts, many have asked if such programs can make a difference. The evidence is clear: They can.

More tobacco control correlates with less tobacco use.

The stakes are high. Tobacco use kills more Americans each year than any other cause. The estimated 430,000 deaths attributed to tobacco use annually are far more than those caused by illegal drugs, homicides, suicides, AIDS, motor vehicle accidents, and alcohol combined. Lung cancer kills more Americans than breast and prostate cancer combined, and tobacco accounts for over 30% of all cancer deaths and a comparable fraction of deaths due to heart and lung diseases. Yet despite these risks, many, many people start smoking each year. In 1996, over 1.8 million people became daily smokers, two-thirds of them (1.2 million) under age 18.

Over the past decade, states have moved to the forefront of tobacco control. Starting with California in 1988, and followed by Massachusetts, Arizona, Oregon, and other states, referenda have increased tobacco excise taxes and dedicated a fraction of the revenues to reducing tobacco use. Legislatures in other states—such as Alaska, Hawaii, Maryland, Michigan, New Jersey, New York, and Washington—have increased tobacco taxes substantially, raising questions about how much of the revenue should go to tobacco control. In addition, settlements of lawsuits against tobacco firms to recoup state monies spent through Medicaid have now resulted in individual state revenue streams (in Florida, Minnesota, Mississippi, and Texas) or in revenues through the Master Settlement Agreement with the other states and territories signed in 1998. In aggregate, these agreements transferred as much as $246 billion from tobacco firms to states over the next 25 years.

State programs make a difference

The best evidence for the effectiveness of state tobacco control programs comes from comparing states with different intensities of tobacco control, as measured by funding levels and "aggressiveness." For example, when California and Massachusetts mounted programs that were more "intense" than those of other states, they showed greater decreases in tobacco use compared to states that were part of the American Stop Smoking Intervention Study (ASSIST) funded by the National Cancer Institute. From 1989 to 1993, when the Massachusetts program began, California had the largest and most aggressive tobacco control program in the nation, and it showed a singular decline in cigarette consumption that was over 50%

faster than the national average. A recent evaluation of the Massachusetts tobacco control program showed a 15% decline in adult smoking—compared to very little change nationally—thus reducing the number of smokers there by 153,000 between 1993 and 1999. States that were part of the ASSIST program, in turn, devoted more resources to tobacco control than did other states except Massachusetts and California, and they showed in aggregate a 7% reduction in tobacco consumption per capita from 1993 to 1996 compared to non-ASSIST states. Such a "dose-response" effect is strong evidence that state programs have an impact; that more tobacco control correlates with less tobacco use, and that the reduction coincides with the intensification of tobacco control efforts.

A second line of evidence comes from observing effects on tobacco consumption beyond those associated with price. When tobacco prices rise, sales should drop, and when prices drop, sales should rise. Yet price alone does not explain the observed consumption patterns. In the first 2 years after Oregon's ballot initiative was implemented, for example, cigarette consumption dropped by over 11%, which is 5% more than would be expected from the price increase alone. The recently reported decreases in tobacco use in Alaska, California, and Florida similarly exceed what would be expected from price increases alone. Moreover, when cigarette prices dropped nationwide during 1992–1994, consumption rose in states with small tobacco control efforts but did not rise in 11 of 14 ASSIST states; consumption also plateaued in California and Massachusetts. This suggests that tobacco control measures limited the increase in tobacco sales expected as a result of a price drop.

In the review of tobacco control program elements that follows, results are reported in ranges, and sometimes those ranges are large. It is generally quite difficult to attribute a reduction in tobacco use to any single factor; often, many factors work in parallel. The underlying message is quite clear, however: Multifaceted state tobacco control programs are effective in reducing tobacco use.

Counteradvertising and education

Counteradvertising and public education campaigns have become standard elements of tobacco control, although their funding levels and aggressiveness vary considerably among the states. Counteradvertising campaigns can convey a variety of messages and can be aimed at different audiences. An evaluation of the California tobacco control program concluded that it was most effective in its early years, when the highest-impact advertisements emphasized deceptive practices undertaken by tobacco firms. Evaluators concluded that the program became less effective when spending for counteradvertising dropped (from $16 million in 1991 to $6.6 million by 1995), and when the advertisements began to focus on health risks rather than tobacco industry practices. As a result, the program's advisory committee made its foremost 1997 goal to "vigorously expose tobacco industry tactics." A "natural experiment" under way in Florida may provide further insight. The Florida Pilot Program, funded by that state's tobacco settlement, created the edgy "Truth Campaign" and SWAT (Students Working Against Tobacco) program. During its first year, tobacco use among youths decreased dramatically. The second-year budgets for both programs were seriously threatened in the Florida legislature—at one point facing extinction—but funding was partially restored. The program director was removed and the counteradvertising campaign was said to be heading "in a new direction." The budget for public media is slated to drop from $24 million to $18 million in the second year. If the rate of decline in tobacco consumption among youths stalls in Florida, as it did in California after 1994, this would provide further evidence that the "dose" of tobacco control predicts its impact.

School-based tobacco prevention programs are also part of state tobacco control programs. The effectiveness of school-based programs varies. They are most effective when the message is delivered repeatedly and is taken as seriously and promoted as powerfully as are other forms of drug abuse education. Properly implemented school programs can, however, lower smoking prevalence from 25% to 60%. These programs have been evaluated repeatedly, and in 1994 CDC [Centers for Disease Control and Prevention] produced a set of guidelines for school-based programs. States will want to take care in implementing school-based programs, however, because they can consume considerable resources to little effect; a 1996 meta-analysis showed only a modest impact for most programs. The 1994 Institute of Medicine report *Growing Up Tobacco Free* noted the variable results of school-based programs but concluded that they should be part of a comprehensive tobacco control strategy because educating school-age children and adolescents about the consequences of tobacco use is clearly important to sustain a smoke-free norm.

> *Raising the price of tobacco products through taxation is one of the fastest ways to discourage children and youths from starting to smoke.*

Experimentation with the content and style of counteradvertising and education programs will and should continue, subject to evaluation to enable improvements and increase their impact. With that in mind, the American Legacy Foundation has been established with funding from the Master Settlement Agreement. Its duties include funding and oversight of a national counteradvertising campaign. Many states have also increased their counteradvertising and education initiatives.

Establishing smoke-free workplaces and public spaces

The main impetus for smoke-free environments grew from concern about exposing nonsmokers to the toxic effects of tobacco smoke. Making worksites, schools, and homes smoke-free zones is a powerful strategy for reducing tobacco use overall because it boosts quit rates and reduces consumption. A 1996 review, for example, estimated that smoke-free workplaces reduced the number of smokers by 5% on average (meaning that almost one in five smokers quit, as smoking prevalence is about 25%) and reduced use among continuing smokers by 10%. Another review attributed over 22% of the tobacco consumption drop in Australia between 1988 and 1995, and almost 13% of the drop in the United States between

1988 and 1994, to smoke-free workplace policies. The death toll and ill-health attributable to involuntary smoking are thoroughly documented in a Surgeon General's report, a report from the federal Environmental Protection Agency (EPA), and a study by the California EPA. Federal regulations prohibit smoking in federal buildings and in airplanes. In some states and localities, laws and ordinances proscribe smoking in workplaces, schools, public spaces, restaurants, and other sites. Creating smoke-free workplaces and public spaces reduces tobacco use among smokers while reducing involuntary smoking by nonsmokers. Smoking restrictions have been a major focus of some states' tobacco control efforts and are a central thrust of much activity at the county and city levels.

Increasing prices through taxation

Raising the price of tobacco products through taxation is one of the fastest and most effective ways to discourage children and youths from starting to smoke and to encourage smokers to quit. In 1994 and 1998, the Institute of Medicine recommended price increases of $2 per pack (or equivalent for other tobacco products), based on levels needed to approach the health goals in *Healthy People 2000* and to approach parity with other countries that have effective tobacco control programs. Wholesale prices have increased an average of $0.65 per pack nationwide since the Master Settlement Agreement was signed in 1998, the federal excise tax was raised to $0.24 per pack in the Balanced Budget Act of 1997, and six states now have excise taxes over $0.75 per pack. Even high-tax states remain short of the Institute's recommended level, however, and 20 states have excise taxes below $0.20 per pack. The wholesale price and excise tax increases do not necessarily imply equal increases in retail prices that consumers see, as discounts to retailers are commonplace for tobacco products, and local business factors are important. It is nonetheless clear that the floor for prices has risen, even if the ceiling is variable.

Economists have reached a consensus that a cigarette price increase of 10% will decrease total consumption by about 4%. Most economists now believe the response is larger (i.e., about 8%) among youths, based on recent studies. Conclusions about whether price disproportionately affects children and youths are based on fewer data than larger studies of total tobacco consumption. A classic 1990 study showed that responsiveness to price (elasticity of demand) increased over time from 1970 to 1985 but found little difference between adults and youths. A more recent review of more elaborate studies showed elasticities in the range noted above; it also found that youths were more sensitive to price, as demonstrated by fewer youths starting to smoke and reduced consumption among continuing youth smokers. An April 1998 report from the Congressional Budget Office reviewed many studies of price and consumption. It found unequivocal evidence that increased prices reduce use, although details about the mechanisms and effects are not completely understood.

Proposals to increase cigarette taxes face strong opposition. (Interestingly, tobacco taxes are one of the few taxes for which a majority of Americans favor increases, especially if the revenues derived are dedicated to tobacco control.) The principal policy concern is that tobacco taxes are regressive, because tobacco use is more common among people with low incomes, and thus the poor spend proportionately more of their incomes on cigarettes. Tax increases are actually less regressive than simple projections suggest, however, because the poor are more sensitive to price and their consumption falls more sharply when prices rise. The World Bank supports increasing tobacco excise taxes for its public health impact and notes that judgments about regressiveness "should be over the distributional impact of the entire tax and expenditure system, and less on particular taxes in isolation."

Governors and legislators have raised concerns about increasing prices on tobacco because revenues from excise taxes might drop, along with payments expected under the Master Settlement Agreement (because payments to states are tied to sales). States concerned about revenue loss have an effective option—raising the state excise tax rate. The World Bank notes that "empirical evidence shows that raised tobacco taxes bring greater [overall] tobacco tax revenues." Reduced consumption will also ultimately lead to lower health costs to states through Medicaid and other health programs. In one study, the health benefits due to lower rates of heart attack and stroke began quickly, and the health benefits more than offset the program's costs after 1 year. The immediate economic and health benefits are later compounded by reductions in cancer and other chronic diseases.

Supporting treatment programs for tobacco dependence

Nicotine addiction, like other addictions, is a treatable condition. Treatment programs for tobacco dependence can work. States have two major roles in treating tobacco dependence: (1) educating tobacco-dependent people about their treatment options through public health programs, and (2) ensuring that medical programs cover and reimburse the costs of the treatments. As of 1997, only 22 states and the District of Columbia covered such treatment under Medicaid, leading to a recommendation that state Medicaid agencies "incorporate explicit language into their managed-care contracts, policy briefs, lawsuit provisions, and Medicaid formularies." States can take guidance on policies to improve tobacco treatments from a report by the Center for the Advancement of Health.

Community-based resources such as centralized "quitlines" and workplace wellness programs can increase access to cessation programs. State governments are among the largest employers in most states, and a major employer in all. States can ensure that their employees have access to treatment through their health plans, and smoking bans in state buildings can increase cessation and reduce tobacco use among continuing smokers. States can also pass laws to create smoke-free businesses, public buildings, and worksites. State and local media campaigns that reinforce nonsmoking norms also enhance motivation to quit, reduce tobacco use among those who continue to smoke, and prevent relapse.

Much can be done to improve access to and the effectiveness of treatment programs within medical systems. More than 70% of smokers visit a primary health care provider at least once a year. Systematic reviews conclude that routine, repeated advice and support can increase smoking cessation rates by 2- to 3-fold. Physicians, nurses, psychologists, dentists, and other health professionals are more likely to give such advice and support if they practice in a system that encourages such behavior through practice-based systems for tracking smoking status, office-based written materials for smokers to take home, training of health professionals in screening and advising patients, coverage of cessation programs by health plans, and reimbursement for treatments by payers (including Medicaid).

Enforcing laws against sales to minors can reduce tobacco consumption.

Most people who use tobacco—at all ages—express a desire to quit, but only a small fraction succeed on their own. Although many who do quit do so without formal treatment, treatment clearly improves cessation rates. Controlled studies generally report 30%–35% cessation rates at 1 year for intensive treatments and 10%–20% cessation rates for less-intensive treatments. Treatment for addiction to tobacco products ranks high in cost-effectiveness among health program spending options. Programs that combine behavioral therapies with pharmacotherapies (i.e., medications) have the best results, and evidence-based guidelines recommend that all smokers should be offered both. Behavioral programs can be delivered in group settings (in person) or individually (in person or by telephone). FDA-approved medications include nicotine replacement agents (in gum, patch, nasal spray, or inhaler delivery systems) and the antidepressant drug bupropion.

Treatment works, but there is ample room for improvement. Despite evidence of its effectiveness, relatively few smokers seek out formal treatment, and relapse rates are high. Improving smoking cessation success rates would be especially important in certain target populations. For example, Massachusetts placed an emphasis on reducing smoking among pregnant women because it would produce long-lasting benefits for the prospective mothers and reduce risks to their children. As a result, the number of mothers who smoked during pregnancy dropped by almost 48% during 1990–1996, a rate far ahead [of] that of any other state.

Enforcing youth access restrictions

It has long been illegal—in every state—to sell tobacco products to minors, but until recently, enforcement was lax. The federal Synar Amendment ties federal block grant monies to improved compliance with state laws proscribing such sales. States risk reduced payments from the Substance Abuse and Mental Health Administration if they fail to meet compliance targets. The federal government has never withheld state funds based on the Synar Amendment, but such withholding is under discussion for several states that have not met Synar targets. Enforcement of youth sales, with mandatory ID-card inspection of those 26 and younger, was the central thrust of a 1996 FDA tobacco regulation. This part of the regulation remains in force pending a U.S. Supreme Court ruling about FDA's jurisdiction over tobacco products. States now have FDA contracts to enforce and monitor youth sales. Several reports have noted that enforcing laws against sales to minors can reduce tobacco consumption. Although one 1997 study of enforcement showed no decline in youth smoking, the authors attributed the lack of impact to insufficient merchant compliance and developed a model approach that is being used in Massachusetts. Excessive focus or exclusive reliance on youth access restrictions can siphon resources and political will from more powerful tobacco control measures. Yet all U.S. jurisdictions have youth access laws, and if those laws are to become meaningful, they must be enforced.

Monitoring performance and evaluating programs

Today's tobacco control programs build on decades of research and demonstrations. The scale and scope of tobacco control in the United States—particularly in the most aggressive states—has grown considerably over the past decade, and the proper balance and content of program elements are the subjects of continuing debate. Tobacco control can improve over time only if (a) its elements are assessed, (b) state programs that choose different strategies are compared, and (c) research to improve the programs is carried out. Governors and state legislators, moreover, need to be able to be accountable for the use of public dollars. This does not imply that results will be quick; significant reductions in tobacco use take years even in states where tobacco control has clearly been effective.

Performance monitoring of public health programs is receiving increased attention. Measures to monitor the performance of tobacco control programs are in place, and efforts are under way to improve them. Without specified goals and ways of measuring progress, the effectiveness of public monies spent on such programs is hard to judge, so state tobacco control programs should include resources for evaluation and research as part of a comprehensive tobacco control program.

8

Government Antismoking Campaigns Are Socialist Propaganda

Vic Bilson

Vic Bilson is the editor of the Jeremiah Project, an online Christian "print ministry" that posts views on numerous religious and social issues.

Smokers are stripped of their civil rights, denied employment rights, and reduced to second-class citizens as the government increasingly works to make smoking illegal in public places. The government's antismoking campaigns pretend to focus on health, drug abuse, or teen smoking, but these campaigns are mere socialist propaganda. The government is actually interested in making money and controlling the lives of its citizens. Legislation slated to reduce teen smoking, for example, does nothing more than raise taxes on the middle class, extending the role of government in private lives. Exaggerations about the negative health effects of tobacco lead to higher insurance premiums and medical fees. And antismoking sentiment has led to a decline in personal responsibility, as members of society find means for blaming smoking-related problems on someone else.

What began in 1971 as a minor inconvenience to air traveling smokers has turned more recently into one of the wildest feeding frenzies for lawmakers and attorneys everywhere and an erosion of liberty for all Americans.

In 1971, United Airlines introduced separate sections for smokers and nonsmokers on their airplanes followed by the first federal restriction on smoking in public places in 1973 when the Civil Aeronautics Board required all airlines to create nonsmoking sections. Fifteen years later, in 1988, Congress banned smoking on domestic flights of less than two hours. Today, not only is smoking banned on domestic and international flights, smoking is also banned inside most airports.

The Federal government extended its reach in the fray, supported by trial lawyers, with their eyes on huge repositories of money to extend the reach of government and fund their big government programs. It has now become politically correct to discriminate against smokers socially with isolation and ridiculing behavior, and economically with higher taxes and other costs.

The result has been that smokers have systematically been stripped of their civil rights, denied their employment rights, and reduced to second class citizens as smoking has been made illegal in most public places.

Smoking Aloud will attempt to clear the smoke from the controversial issues while probing the various claims made by the Socialist led anti-smoking movement. We will also consider the longer-term consequences of the ensuing legislative and litigative activity as well as develop the thesis that . . . The ongoing anti-smoking campaign is not about public health, drug abuse, or teen smoking. What it is all about is money, control, and jurisdiction.

Deception #1: public health

Central to any socialist movement is the idea that whatever a bureaucracy does is for the "public good." Hence, we have seen the rise of phrases like, "health care crisis," "pediatric crisis," and some of their most persuasive rhetoric, "it's for the children," and "it's the right thing to do." It's been said that if you tell a lie often enough, people will eventually believe it. Today, a growing number of uninformed and simple minded Americans have bought into the lies.

There may be a health care crisis, but not the kind these Socialists are wanting you to believe. Rising costs in our health care system and the drain on Medicare is not caused by smokers . . . it's caused by the explosion of an AIDS epidemic among the homosexual and intravenous drug user community. Insurance rates aren't skyrocketing because of health care costs for smokers . . . it's caused by out of control health care costs of homosexual domestic partners with AIDS. Major corporation after corporation has begun extending health care coverage to homosexual couples in the battle against AIDS.

Passive or secondhand smoke is not causing cancer in anybody today.

With a contrived crisis as its centerpiece, government and social propagandists have sprung into action with elaborate public relations campaigns whipping the public into a frightened frenzy where they willingly and blindly submit themselves to a money and power hungry cadre of statists. Both Democrats and Republicans in Congress, pushed on by President [Bill] Clinton, have proposed sham legislation that does nothing for public health, does not address their stated goals of reducing teen smoking, but rather raises taxes on the middle-class and extends the size and authority of government over private lives.

In addition to individual settlements with Mississippi, Florida, Texas and Minnesota, the tobacco industry and state attorneys general reached agreement in November, 1998, to settle litigation brought by the attorneys general in the remaining states and jurisdictions. Including the four individual state settlements, the industry has agreed to pay a total of $246 billion to the states, end all outdoor advertising and severely restrict other traditional marketing practices, and fund a national research foundation and a public education campaign.

What's been their rationale supporting their grab for money and power? Fear, fear, and more distorted fear! It's the same process the government used in an earlier time with their "Reefer Madness" propaganda. Nearly all the recent tobacco legislation has been based on bogus and discredited research.

In the '60's they told us that taking a toke off that marijuana cigarette turned people into sex crazed murderers. Today they tell us that people who light up in public and puff on their cigarettes not only put themselves at risk but also are causing cancer in those non-smokers around them.

Well, the fact is that marijuana smokers were not transformed into sex crazed killers in the 1960's and passive or secondhand smoke is not causing cancer in anybody today.

So, why are we being told these lies?

Read on and I'll try to explain it to you.

Agendas and deceptions

Agenda #1: MONEY.

The current propaganda campaign being waged against the tobacco industry amounts to extortion by the U.S. government, trial lawyers, insurance companies, and many others in the health related professions. They are simply coercing your money from you through the spreading of fear and in some cases lying to you in exchange for higher taxes, huge legal fees, higher insurance premiums, and higher medical fees. Not-for-profit public health organizations have their hands out as well, seeing an almost endless supply of money to fund their research grants. Make no mistake about it—MONEY is the foundational issue. Take money out of the equation and these bleeding heart liberals will tuck their tails and abandon your children.

Deception #2: DRUG ABUSE.

Illegal drug use has increased substantially under the leadership of the Clinton administration. This increase is without considering tobacco as a drug, rather [it] considers only highly addictive drugs like cocaine and heroin, or Clinton's favorite, marijuana. In the wake of his failed policies concerning dangerous addictive drugs, President Clinton has again pulled a SLICK maneuver and has successfully "redefined" tobacco as an addictive drug in a deceptive ploy to make it look like he is doing something about drugs. But, drug use is not reduced—only new federal regulations are imposed on legal businesses through an expanded Food and Drug Administration.

Agenda #2: CONTROL.

The rise of the anti-smoking sentiment in America coincides with society's move from personal responsibility to attaching blame for just about everything on someone or something else other than where the true blame resides. Along with abandoning personal responsibility, "enlightened" Americans have renounced reason and truth and have handed over the control of their lives to a power hungry conglomerate of rich politicians, lawyers, and doctors.

Relishing the idea of broader government reach into private lives, law makers have gladly provided the structure whereby government becomes the savior and caretaker of the people. Using the Environmental Protection Agency (EPA) as its propaganda arm, the federal government has used sham research to empower state and local authorities to restrict smoking in public places, including offices, restaurants and commercial airliners. Along with expanded government control of private lives comes the associated bloated budgets and rising taxes to pay for it all.

Deception #3: TEEN SMOKING.

To win your hearts and minds, anti-smokers have launched massive deceptive public relations campaigns much like the "Reefer Madness" campaign and are manipulating public policy in the interest of big government. Several years ago they discovered through focus group studies that people react positively to their message if the emphasis is more on children—hence the "It's for the children" propaganda.

Agenda #3: JURISDICTION.

Authoritarian and totalitarian regimes—be they fascist or communist in nature—have always sought to destroy the traditional family unit by severing the bonds between parents and their children, thereby increasing the power of the government. Adolf Hitler understood that if he were to control the German people, he had to first control the children. He started by first taking charge of the children and educating them to follow his racist view and teaching them that it was ok to kill and torture Jews, and anyone that shared different ideals. Before it was over, Hitler's youth were even turning in their parents if they shared other values.

Today, the target of their Socialist agenda is still the children and the intact family is still their greatest enemy. Our kids' minds are being filled with every imaginable distortion of reality by the NEA [National Education Association] led public school system and it's not too far off before "child welfare" officials will find the legal precedent to remove children from their homes if their parents are smokers. After all, in Hillary Clinton's words, "It takes more than a family to raise children."

9

Television Viewing May Encourage Youth Smoking

Pradeep P. Gidwani et al.

Pradeep P. Gidwani is affiliated with the Center for Child Health Outcomes at the Children's Hospital and Health Center in San Diego, California. He is especially involved in efforts to assess how well states are addressing the needs of children with chronic health conditions.

Although government bans prevent tobacco advertising on television, the act of smoking is still often depicted in television shows and televised sporting events. This study finds that youths who watch a greater amount of television than their peers are more likely to begin smoking. Thus, researchers conclude, television viewing should be included as a risk factor in future studies of youth smoking, and efforts to reduce television viewing among youths may reduce the number of youths who begin smoking.

Smoking is the leading preventable cause of death in the United States, and the risk of disease increases the earlier in life smoking begins. Approximately 70% of smokers become regular smokers by age 18. The prevalence of smoking among US adolescents has increased since 1991. Approximately 3 million adolescent smokers consume nearly a billion packs of cigarettes each year. Clearer understanding of the factors that influence the initiation of tobacco use by adolescents may provide opportunities for prevention.

Television programs depicting tobacco usage may encourage smoking among adolescents. Although bans have prevented direct tobacco advertising on television, studies have indicated the widespread portrayal of smoking on television in prime-time programming, movies, music videos, and sporting events. In a recent review of 81 G-rated films, 35 films (43%) showed tobacco use with a mean exposure of 2.1 minutes per film. In music videos, smokers are typically portrayed as attractive, successful, and influential and in a positive social context, often with sexually suggestive content. Rarely is smoking portrayed in an unattractive manner or associated with negative consequences. Logos, billboards, and banners for cigarettes make tobacco advertising a prominent feature of sporting events on American television. Television thereby may serve as an indirect method of smoking advertising.

The premise that television instructs and motivates behavior is grounded in social learning theory. According to this theory, people acquire new skills or behavioral scripts primarily through the observation of models. People perform the behavior in response to expected and valued rewards; these can be rewards that they have earned before or observed being given to others ("vicarious reinforcement"). As noted, television provides adolescents with role models, including movie and television stars and athletes, who portray smoking as a personally and socially rewarding behavior.

The association between smoking and television

No longitudinal studies have examined the association between smoking and television exposure. Because adolescents are heavy watchers of television, we hypothesized that youth with greater exposure to television viewing would exhibit higher incidence of smoking initiation.

We used the National Longitudinal Survey of Youth, Child Cohort (NLSY), to examine longitudinally the association of television viewing in 1990 with smoking initiation between 1990 and 1992.

The original NLSY cohort is composed of a nationally representative sample of youth aged 14 to 21 years in 1979. Individuals in the cohort were interviewed in person annually since 1979. Although the focus of the NLSY is labor force–related behavior, the annual interviewer-administered questionnaires provide extensive information on health. The NLSY oversampled African American, Hispanic-American, and poor non-Hispanic white populations. Beginning in 1986, data on the children of women in this original cohort were collected, and these children form the basis for the sample in this study. Additional description of this cohort can be found in a study on obesity and television viewing. We analyzed the responses of youth who were 10 to 15 years of age in 1990; they were still <18 years of age in 1992 and therefore below the legal age to purchase cigarettes in a majority of states. We excluded children without complete reports of television viewing and missing information about smoking. The final sample consists of 592 individuals.

We classified youth who reported smoking in the last 3 months as having initiated smoking behaviors. Individuals who reported smoking in 1990 were excluded from the analysis because of the focus on smoking initiation. We relied on self-report of smoking behavior. . . .

Hours of television viewing and controls

The NLSY provides information for television viewing based on the youth report alone, the parent report alone, and the average of the youth and parent reports. . . . We used the average score in the analyses, based on the assumption that the combined score of 2 reporters would be more reliable and valid than a single report. Television viewing was categorized into: 0 to 2, >2 to 3, >3 to 4, >4 to 5, and >5 hours per day. Because the American Academy of Pediatrics recommends limiting television viewing to no more than 2 hours per day, youth who watched <2 hours per day served as the reference group.

We controlled for several socioeconomic and demographic factors (ethnicity, household poverty, marital status, number of children in the household), maternal factors (education, measured intelligence, employment), and child factors (gender and baseline child aptitude test scores). Ethnicity was categorized as white non-Hispanic, black, or Hispanic. Household poverty was dichotomized as above or below 100% of the federal poverty line in 1990. Mother's marital status was dichotomized into married or not married in 1990. Maternal intelligence was measured by the Armed Forces Qualification Test in 1986. Maternal employment was categorized as employed or unemployed in 1990. Child aptitude test scores were measured by the Peabody Individual Achievement Test for math and reading and the Peabody Picture Vocabulary Test. . . .

More likely to smoke

In 1990, the mean age of the cohort was 11.5 years with a range of 10 to 15. In 1990, 34 individuals reported smoking in the last 3 months. They were excluded from the cohort. In 1992, an additional 57 individuals reported smoking behaviors. When youth who initiated smoking behaviors were compared with youth who did not initiate smoking behaviors, no significant difference was found based on gender, age, maternal education, household poverty, maternal marriage status, or number of children.

Television . . . may serve as an indirect method of smoking advertising.

The percentage of youth smoking in the cohort increased from 4.8% in 1990 to 12.3% in 1992. The average amount of television viewing in 1990 was 4.8 hours per day. Approximately one third of youth watched >5 hours of television per day, and one tenth of youth watched 0 to 2 hours per day. Of the individuals who initiated smoking in 1992, 42% viewed television for >5 hours per day.

We examined the relationship between television viewing and initiation of smoking and found a strong dose-response relationship with increasing hours (Table 1). Controlling for baseline characteristics, youth who watched >5 hours of television per day were 5.99 times more likely to initiate smoking behaviors than those youth who watched 0–2 hours per day. Similarly, youth who watched >4 to 5 hours per day were 5.24 times more likely to initiate smoking than youth who watched 0–2 hours. Although the associations between smoking initiation and youth who watch >2 to 3 hours and >3 to 4 hours were not statistically significant, a clear trend is visible. Youth who watched >2 to 3 hours were 2.00 times more likely to initiate smoking behaviors, and youth who watched >3 to 4 hours were 3.15 times more likely to initiate smoking behaviors when compared with youth who watched 0 to 2 hours per day.

We found significant associations between smoking initiation and race/ethnicity, household structure, and poverty. African American and

Table 1: Percentage of Smoking Initiation Between 1990 and 1992 by Amount of Television Viewed Per Day in 1990

Hours of Television Viewing Per Day (1990)	Percentage of Subjects Who Initiated Smoking
0–2	4.8
>2–3	5.1
>3–4	8.8
>4–5	14.2
>5	12.9

Hispanic-American youth were less likely to initiate smoking behaviors than their white counterparts. Youth who lived in a household where their mother was married were half as likely to initiate smoking as youth whose mother was not married. Finally, youth whose families lived in poverty were more likely to initiate smoking behaviors.

A significant association

These results indicate a significant dose-response association between television viewing and youth smoking initiation. The direction of the relationship supports the hypothesis that exposure to images of smoking on television may increase the likelihood of smoking initiation in youth. A similar association between television viewing and the onset of alcohol use has been reported, with each additional hour of television viewing associated with a 9% average increase in the initiation of drinking.

The incidence of smoking in our analysis is consistent with previous epidemiologic research. In 1992, the incidence of smoking in our cohort was 10.2%. When we included youth who were already smoking in 1990, the total prevalence of smoking behaviors was 12.3% in 1992. That same year, the Monitoring the Future Study, a nationally representative sample, found that 15.5% of eighth-graders had used cigarettes in the last 30 days. In addition, the incidence of smoking among minority groups in our cohort was consistent with data from other studies.

Limitations of the study

This study has several major limitations. Although our estimates describe a strong prospective association of television viewing with smoking initiation, these are not experimental data. We have no direct evidence that changing television-viewing time will produce changes in smoking initiation, these are not experimental data. We have no direct evidence that changing television-viewing time will produce changes in smoking initiation. Because this is a nonexperimental epidemiologic study, we need to be mindful of other threats to the validity of making inferences regarding causality. Criteria for assessing causality in nonexperimental studies include these: 1) the causal exposure must clearly precede the hypothesized outcome; 2) the association should be strong and consistent; 3) the association should be specific; 4) there should be evidence of exposure response; and 5) the association should be expected from theory. The longitudinal nature of the NLSY cohort provides temporal sequence; in this study, television viewing was measured 2 years before smoking initiation. The association was substantial, with youth who watched >5 hours per day being 5.99 times as likely to initiate smoking than youth who watched 0 to 2 hours per day. Evidence of exposure response is seen in the dose-dependent association between smoking initiation and television viewing. Finally, the findings are consistent with social learning theory. Youth view positive images of smoking on television in prime-time programming, movies, music videos, and sporting events.

Of the individuals who initiated smoking in 1992, 42% viewed television for [more than five] hours a day.

Three other limitations include the following: we were unable to examine the effects of peer smoking because the NLSY did not include that variable. Second, the NLSY provides information only on hours of television viewing without information on the content or type of television exposure. Exactly what adolescents watch may matter a great deal. T.N. Robinson and colleagues found an association of television and music video viewing with increased onset of alcohol use in adolescents, whereas videocassette viewing was associated with a decreased onset of alcohol use. Third, we do not have information on other media use, e.g., magazines, Internet, etc.

The association of television viewing and incidence of smoking in this sample could reflect the influence of other unmeasured variables. However, we did control for many of the variables found to be associated with both television viewing and smoking incidence among youth, including ethnicity, household income poverty, and school performance.

Television viewing has negative effects

TV viewing may serve as a marker for youth who exhibit high-risk behaviors such as smoking. R. Jessor notes that different risk behaviors may cluster together in adolescents because they serve a function related to social or psychological development, including identity formation and achieving adult status. Several researchers have shown a clustering of risk behaviors. L.G. Escobedo et al demonstrated an association between cigarette smoking and other health risk and problem behaviors. R.H. DuRant et al found that early age of onset of cigarette smoking was the strongest correlate of the overall number of risk behaviors in a group of middle-school students. Although current work focused on the clustering of adolescent risk behaviors has included smoking, television viewing has not been included as a risk factor.

Alternatively, television viewing may substitute for activities that build resilience and help youth guard against high-risk behaviors. Recent resilience research has demonstrated that bonding to family and school is a protective factor for a broad range of health-risk behaviors in adolescents. Television viewing by youth may reduce family bonding by decreasing interaction between parents and adolescents. J.D. Hawkins et al reported that an intensive intervention to increase school bonding among elementary school children reduced violent behavior, heavy drinking, and sexual intercourse at 18 years of age. They found no difference in smoking initiation, but the intervention did not include decreasing hours of TV viewing.

This study indicates a strong association of television viewing with higher rates of smoking initiation among youth. Indeed, the pattern of results suggests that television, with its frequent positive portrayals of smoking, may be an effective indirect method of tobacco promotion. These results should alert parents, educators, and health professionals to the possibility that active efforts to discourage television viewing by youth may be an effective strategy for reducing the incidence of smoking and possibly other high-risk behaviors with which it is correlated.

10

Contemporary Films Often Advertise Tobacco Brands

James D. Sargent et al.

Dr. James D. Sargent is associate professor in the Department of Pediatrics and Adolescent Medicine and the Department of Community and Family Medicine at Dartmouth-Hitchcock Medical Center in Lebanon, New Hampshire. His current research involves evaluating media and marketing influences on adolescent smoking.

After assessing 250 top box-office films from 1988 to 1997, researchers discovered tobacco use in more than 85 percent of these films. Tobacco brand appearances were common even in films rated for children, and findings suggest an increase in on-screen actor-endorsement of cigarette brands. The fact that the top four U.S. cigarette brands appear most frequently in contemporary films suggests that brand advertising is the motive for tobacco product placement in films.

The visual presentation of brands in cinema films is generally thought of as a form of advertising, which is pursued by companies because it influences people to purchase or use a product. Brand placement in films has become a preferred method for companies to raise brand awareness and develop favourable associations with their products for an international audience. Case reports suggest that this practice can be effective in promoting sales. Increasingly, brand placement in films is part of an integrated international marketing plan for corporate products, such as the deal between beer, spirits, car, and mobile-phone manufacturers, plus a credit-card company in the film *Tomorrow Never Dies*. In total, these companies spent almost US$98 million worldwide in advertisements associated with the release of this movie, which also featured their products.

Although there have been several studies of tobacco use in films, we identified only one mention of tobacco-brand appearances in films. T.F. Stockwell and S.A. Glantz assessed a random sample of five of the top 20 box-office hits for each year from 1985 to 1995, and noted that brand appearances declined after 1990, although these findings were not supported by any data. Moreover, if brand appearances are fairly uncommon, trend analysis by sampling only five movies per year would be difficult.

We investigated the frequency of tobacco-brand appearances in the top 25 US box-office hits per year for 10 years (1988–97). We aimed to assess trends in relation to a tobacco-industry ban on payments for brand placement in films, and to estimate the size of the international audience for films with cigarette-brand appearances.

We selected the top 25 box-office hits in the USA for every year from 1988 to 1997 (250 in total) obtained from the website www.worldwideboxoffice.com on March 1, 1998 (accessed on Dec. 14, 2000). We analysed the content to assess the association between exposure to tobacco use in films and smoking behaviour in a sample of US adolescents.

Use of tobacco by an adolescent's favourite actor has been associated with the smoking behaviour of the adolescent.

In addition to describing brand appearances, we assessed whether the frequency and type of brand appearance had changed since the tobacco industry incorporated a ban into its voluntary advertising code on payments for brand placement in films in 1989. Since it takes about 1 year for movies to be released after the production stages, we thought that many of the films released in 1990 would have been produced before the ban. Therefore we classified films released in 1988–90 as released before the ban and those produced in 1991–97 as released after the ban.

Tobacco appears in films in many forms

We defined tobacco-brand appearances as the appearance of a brand name, logo, or identifiable trademark on products or product packaging, billboards, store-front advertising, or tobacco promotional items. We defined them as brand appearances because we have no evidence that payments made by the tobacco industry prompted placement in the film (brand placements). Tobacco-brand appearances were coded as actor endorsements when a major or minor actor was using tobacco, or as background appearances when the product's presence on screen was unrelated to characters' behaviour. We distinguished types of appearance because use of tobacco by an adolescent's favourite actor has been associated with the smoking behaviour of the adolescent. Actor endorsement links the brand with a film star and could have a greater effect on smoking behaviour than a background-brand appearance. Additionally, the film industry makes this distinction in negotiations for brand placement. For example, in the film *Mr. Destiny*, Walt Disney Studios charged advertisers $20,000 for showing a product, $40,000 to show a product and have an actor mention the product name, and $60,000 for an actor to be shown using a product. Moreover, reports by lawyers who broker agreements between companies and the film industry show that background brand placement does not generally gain large fees, but if the product constitutes an important element in the story line or is featured prominently during one or more scenes, a substantial fee (possibly several hundred thousand US dollars) may be paid by the manufacturer for the placement. . . .

Only a few films in the sample were rated for general audiences, the rest had parental guidance warnings (US PG, PG-13 film code) or were restricted to audiences aged 17 years or older (US R film code). The films represented several genres, mainly comedies, dramas, and action adventure. Most of the films were set in the contemporary period (from 1990 to present, table).

Characteristic	Number/percentage
MPAA rating	**of films made**
G	11 (4%)
PG	64 (26%)
PG-13	75 (30%)
R	100 (40%)
Genre	
Action adventure	48 (19%)
Animation or children's fantasy	21 (8%)
Comedy	79 (32%)
Drama	56 (22%)
Horror	9 (4%)
Mystery	20 (8%)
Science fiction	17 (7%)
Time-period setting	
Before 1930	25 (10%)
1930–64	12 (5%)
1965–89	47 (19%)
1990–present	151 (60%)
Future	9 (4%)
Unable to determine	6 (2%)
Contained tobacco use	
No	33 (13%)
Yes	217 (87%)
Tobacco-brand appearance	
No	180 (72%)
Yes	70 (28%)

MPAA=Motion Picture Association of America; G=General audiences, all ages; PG=Parental guidance suggested for children; PG-13=Parents strongly cautioned that some material might be inappropriate for children; R=Restricted, people younger than 17 years require accompanying adult.

217 (87%) films contained at least one occurrence of tobacco use; 70 (28%) contained at least one brand appearance and 33 of these contained more than one appearance (range 1–14). Tobacco brands were identifiable while actors with major or minor roles were using tobacco in 20 (8%) films. All actor endorsements involved display of the product. Background tobacco-brand appearances were more common than actor endorsements, and were seen in 59 (24%) films. Of these background appearances, 56% involved a display of products, 40% involved a display of logos on clothing or advertising, and 4% involved a verbal mention of tobacco brands.

137 tobacco-brand appearances were seen in 70 films that contained at least one brand appearance. Although 27 tobacco brands were depicted, four cigarette brands accounted for 80% of appearances. Brands did not generally appear for smokeless tobacco, loose tobacco, or cigars.

Tobacco brands appear in films despite a voluntary ban

The frequency of brand appearance in films rated for adult audiences compared with adolescent audiences did not differ (35 *vs* 32%). Popular adolescent-audience films with tobacco-brand appearances included: *Ghostbusters II, Home Alone 2 (Lost in New York), Honey I Shrunk the Kids, Kindergarten Cop, Men in Black, My Best Friend's Wedding, The Nutty Professor,* and *Volcano.* . . .

The overall frequency of brand appearances was similar before and after the voluntary ban on payment for brand placement in films but the type of brand appearance depicted changed. The proportion of films with only actor endorsement increased from 1% before the ban to 6% after. By contrast, the proportion of films containing only background-brand appearances declined after the ban. No film contained actor-endorsed and background-brand appearance before the ban, but 5% contained both after the ban.

Of the 70 films with at least one tobacco brand appearance, we obtained data on US and international box-office revenues for 48 (69%). For these films, revenues outside the USA accounted for 49% of the total revenues earned. The appearance of tobacco brand imagery was not associated with US box-office revenue or the proportion of total revenues earned through international distribution.

Tobacco companies advertise products in US films

Cigarette-brand appearances are common in popular films. The brands that appear most frequently are also the most highly advertised in the USA, which suggests a concordance between the advertising goals of the tobacco industry and the actions of the film industry. Whether or not a financial exchange takes place between the industries, the result is the same: US cigarettes are being marketed to a global audience through cinema films.

Tobacco companies publicly ended direct financial payments for tobacco brand placement in films in 1989, and the top 13 tobacco firms incorporated limits on such payments into their tobacco marketing procedure. Article 7 of this procedure reads: "No payment, direct or indirect, shall be made for the placement of our cigarettes or cigarette advertisements in any film produced for viewing by the general public". Tobacco firms stopped brand placement to avoid Federal regulation. In the USA, at Congress, a bill was introduced that would have made it unlawful in the USA for the manufacturer, packager, or distributor of tobacco products to pay or cause to be paid to have any tobacco product or any tobacco product trademark to appear in any film, music video, television show, play, video arcade game, or other form of entertainment. Despite the regulations on brand placement, we were unable to identify a downward trend in the frequency of tobacco-brand appearances in films. This finding contrasts with the findings of Stockwell and Glantz, who believe that there was a downward trend in brand appearances after 1990. Moreover, our frequency suggests that background-brand placement scenes are being replaced by actor endorsements. Because actor endorsement normally gains payments from companies, this increasing trend suggests an advertising motive behind the appearance of tobacco brands in films.

The frequency of brand appearance in films rated for adult audiences compared with adolescent audiences did not differ.

Several possibilities could explain continued tobacco-brand appearances in films. First, the tobacco industry might continue to pay directly or through in-kind payments for placement of its brands in films. This possibility would be consistent with evidence of regular violation of the Cigarette Advertising Code by the tobacco industry since its inception in 1964. J.W. Richards and colleagues also suggest that amendments to this code have been used to avoid further regulatory oversight on some occasions; a motive is inferred by the timing of the voluntary ban on payments for tobacco-brand placement with attempts in US Congress to regulate the practice of product placement. Second, it might be in the film industry's interest to provide free advertising for tobacco companies. However, how they could do this for one industry without undermining their ability to obtain paid product placements from others is difficult to imagine. Third, brands that are available on the film set could be used without much forethought. For example, because actors use the product on the set the likelihood that it will appear in the film might increase. However, modern films are edited down to the millisecond, and unwanted brand appearances would probably be edited out. Finally, directors might use brand imagery to increase a sense of realism or to convey character traits.

Tobacco-control advocates are concerned about the depiction of tobacco use on screen because of the potential effect it could have on adolescents starting and carrying on smoking. The concern is the same for populations in countries where US tobacco products are heavily marketed, and where people are receptive to the advertising message, for whom films present a seductive, affluent, imaginary world. Through tobacco use on screen, receptive individuals associate stylised, branded smoking behaviour with other elements of US culture. Actor endorsement of a cigarette brand associates a type of person with that brand. As viewers assimilate these images in the context of developing their own smoking identity, their attitudes toward tobacco use become more favourable. Cross-sectional studies show an association between on-screen smoking in an adolescent's favourite movie actor and his or her own smoking behaviour. In respect of these concerns, a ban on tobacco-brand appearances in films seems little different from other advertising restrictions commonly imposed on the tobacco industry, such as bans on billboard advertising.

11

Tobacco Advertising Is Not Solely Responsible for Teen Smoking

Jim Karrh

Jim Karrh is assistant professor of marketing and advertising in the University of Arkansas at Little Rock's College of Business Administration as well as a marketing consultant.

"De-marketing" programs designed to warn teens off smoking can be beneficial, but some of these programs have failed in the past. One reason for this failure is the fact that the decision to begin smoking is fundamentally a social one. Many teens who begin smoking, for instance, believe that smokers are cool and sociable, and they see themselves in the same light. Even teens who admit that smokers are less physically appealing than nonsmokers still view smokers as more rebellious, more cool, and less old-fashioned than nonsmokers. A successful antismoking campaign must not focus on advertising issues alone, but also must address these social signals teens send and receive from smoking.

Can marketing be used to make a product less appealing? Yes, and there's even a name for the practice. "De-marketing" is the strategy of deliberately trying to discourage the purchase or use of a product. The [Arkansas] state Department of Health will soon select a marketing, advertising or public relations firm to help with a tobacco prevention and cessation campaign.

This begs two questions. Can marketing communications from afar really affect teens' smoking choices? And, if so, how exactly could it make a difference?

The evidence says that de-marketing efforts toward tobacco use can be successful. Advertising isn't the biggest factor in influencing teens' buying behavior—surveys suggest that parental influence and peers play bigger roles—but it is still significant. Also, advertising can play a role in reminding parents, school leaders and retailers to be aware, and vigilant.

No ad can actually stop anyone from smoking, but the weight of marketing messages can influence the social context of smoking behavior.

Cigarette smokers were considered less appealing than non-smokers by both males and females.

But there's no guarantee of success, no matter how measured. Teens and preteens are surrounded by brand advertising for cigarettes, cigars and smokeless tobacco. Smoking is prevalent in the media, especially movies; according to a 1994 study in the *American Journal of Public Health*, the rate of smoking in popular movies has consistently been about twice that in the general American population. Even more powerful is the context in which movie smoking occurs—smokers are often portrayed as rebellious, dangerous and, by extension, cool. Think those traits have any appeal to teen-agers?

Tobacco use isn't a rational choice. It's expensive, it excludes you from many places and it carries a host of health problems. The decision to begin smoking must fundamentally be a social one.

The decision to smoke is a social one

Some anti-tobacco campaigns in the past have failed, I believe, because they focus on the wrong goals. A successful campaign in Arkansas won't need to generate awareness or teach health consequences. Everyone, including preteens, is well aware that smoking isn't exactly good for you. Nor should the campaign focus on the tobacco companies, as one national campaign does now. (Do you really think most teens care about tobacco companies—or any company?)

The key is to understand the social signals teens send and receive from smoking. I recently co-authored a study of impressions of smokers that will be published in an upcoming issue of the *Journal of Applied Social Psychology*. In the study, we presented people (primarily 18- and 19-year-olds) photographs of male and female strangers (so there would be no preconceptions), then asked them to rate those strangers on a list of character traits. The photographs were carefully varied—for different experimental subjects, a particular person to rate would be shown holding a cigarette, holding a cigar or holding nothing. In all three cases, the poses were otherwise exactly the same. All other factors were controlled, so any differences in perceptions would be due only to the presence or absence of cigarettes and cigars.

The results? Cigarette smokers were considered less appealing than non-smokers by both males and females. However, cigarette smokers were considered more rebellious, more cool and less old-fashioned. Interestingly, cigar smokers were considered by females to be as appealing as nonsmokers. Further, cigar smokers were judged by both males and females to be the most confident and secure.

Other studies have produced similar results. For example, a study in *Health Psychology*, which tracked fifth- through eighth-graders over time, found that those kids who began smoking tended to relate their image of smokers to their image of themselves. In other words, those kids didn't start smoking to appear more cool or sociable—they began because they believed smokers are cool and sociable and that they were, too. Any effort we make in persuading teens and preteens about smoking must address the perceived link between smokers and "cool."

Personally, I'd rather see tobacco prevention and cessation addressed through persuasion than through more laws or taxes. We have the knowledge, so let's hope this upcoming effort will make a difference.

12

High Schools Should Accommodate Teen Smokers

Madeline Franklin

Madeline Franklin is a sophomore at Williamsville South High School in Buffalo, New York.

In an effort to prevent teen smoking on high school campuses, some school officials lock down student bathrooms when they become filled with cigarette smoke. According to high school student Madeline Franklin, this practice should be discontinued. It is unfair to everyone needing to use the restroom facilities, and teen smoking is likely to continue on campus regardless of locked restrooms. School administrators need to work on a compromise with teen smokers instead of punishing them, such as designating a smoking lounge for students and faculty alike.

Cigarettes and other tobacco products have been popular with adolescents since as long ago as the Civil War. After so many decades, it seems impossible to try to stop teen smoking. However, many schools still try, using methods that students and teachers alike would probably rate as less than effective.

Smoking has never been something for everybody, and due to clean air laws, it is illegal to force someone to endure a smoke-filled environment, hence the choice of "smoking or non" in restaurants. In high schools years ago, students and teachers who wished to smoke were allowed a recreation room, often called a smoking lounge.

After many studies proved smoking to be harmful to health, the general conception was that smoking should be discouraged—thus, no more smoking lounges. But getting rid of the place where smoking takes place on school property does not necessarily mean it will get rid of the smoking on school property.

In a perfect world, kids would always do what they're told (and would always be told to do the right thing). However, this world being far from perfect, kids decided to simply find another place to smoke, the one place where there was no supervision: the bathrooms! Faculty and staff do all they can to bust kids for smoking in the bathrooms, but nevertheless, it continues.

How many of you have walked into a bathroom at your school and walked out reeking of cigarettes? It's unavoidable in high school. And for many, intolerable. There are some people out there who cannot tolerate cigarette smoke.

The most recent and common way to stop the smoking in school bathrooms has been to lock up the bathrooms until there's no more smoke.

There is a better solution

The problems with this "solution" are so apparent that even the staff at some schools laugh at it. Just as humans need clean air, they also need to use the bathroom! Imagine, you've been holding it in for the past three class periods, you finally are allowed to go to the lavatory, but it takes you 10 minutes to even find one that's meant for your gender, and unlocked, but there's already four people waiting!

So maybe this is supposed to put peer pressure on the kids who cause the bathrooms to get locked up to stop smoking in school. If that is the plan, it backfired.

"I can't believe they think that they can stop kids from smoking by not letting us go when we gotta go!" said Marshall S., a sophomore at Williamsville South. Much like taking away the smoking lounges, taking away the bathrooms only leads to innovation. Where are the bathrooms they'd never lock? Faculty bathrooms and locker rooms, also known as, the new place to smoke.

Faculty and staff do all they can to bust kids for smoking in the bathrooms, but nevertheless, it continues.

If smoke in the bathrooms is such a problem, then why not just let students smoke outside? Because state law bans smoking on school property.

A few parents interviewed for this piece suggested that the school might sell a piece of school property to the student body for a "smoking lounge," that would then technically be off school property. Unfortunately, for smokers at least, the anti-tobacco movement has become so strong that it's doubtful anyone would even consider that as an option.

Although the days of smoking lounges seem to be far behind us, smoking is definitely not, despite endless reels of information that positively prove smoking is hazardous to your health. And try as authorities may to stop students from smoking in school, it seems to have little effect. I believe the only real way to solve the problem of smoking in the bathrooms is not to condemn the smokers, but to compromise with them.

Organizations to Contact

The editors have compiled the following list of organizations concerned with the issues debated in this book. The descriptions are derived from materials provided by the organizations. All have publications or information available for interested readers. The list was compiled on the date of publication of the present volume; the information provided here may change. Be aware that many organizations take several weeks or longer to respond to inquiries, so allow as much time as possible.

Action on Smoking and Health (ASH)
2013 H St. NW, Washington, DC 20006
(202) 659-4310
website: www.ash.org

Action on Smoking and Health promotes the rights of nonsmokers and works to protect them from the harms of smoking. ASH worked to eliminate tobacco ads from radio and television and to ban smoking in airplanes, buses, and many public places. The organization publishes the bimonthly newsletter *ASH Smoking and Health Review* and fact sheets on a variety of topics, including teen smoking, passive smoking, and nicotine addiction.

American Cancer Society
1599 Clifton Rd. NE, Atlanta, GA 30329
(800) ACS-2345 (227-2345)
website: www.cancer.org

The American Cancer Society is one of the primary organizations in the United States devoted to educating the public about cancer and funding cancer research. The society spends a great deal of its resources on educating the public about the dangers of smoking and on lobbying for antismoking legislation. The American Cancer Society makes available hundreds of publications, ranging from reports and surveys to position papers.

American Council on Science and Health (ACSH)
1995 Broadway, 2nd Fl., New York, NY 10023-5860
(212) 362-7044 • fax: (212) 362-4919
e-mail: acsh@acsh.org • website: www.acsh.org

ACSH is a consumer education group concerned with issues related to food, nutrition, chemicals, pharmaceuticals, lifestyle, the environment, and health. It publishes the quarterly newsletter *Priorities* as well as the booklets *The Tobacco Industry's Use of Nicotine as a Drug* and *Marketing Cigarettes to Kids*.

Americans for Nonsmokers' Rights
2530 San Pablo Ave., Suite J, Berkeley, CA 94702
(510) 841-3032 • fax: (510) 841-3071
e-mail: anr@no-smoke.org • website: www.no-smoke.org

Americans for Nonsmokers' Rights seeks to protect the rights of nonsmokers in the workplace and other public settings. It works with the American Nonsmokers' Rights Foundation, which promotes smoking prevention, non-smokers' rights, and public education about involuntary smoking. The organization publishes the quarterly newsletter *ANR Update*, the book *Clearing the Air*, and the guidebook *How to Butt In: Teens Take Action.*

Canadian Council for Tobacco Control (CCTC)
170 Laurier Ave. W, Suite 1000, Ottawa, ON K1P 5V5 Canada
(800) 267-5234 • (613) 567-3050 • fax: (613) 567-5695
e-mail: info-services@cctc.ca • website: www.cctc.ca

The CCTC works to ensure a healthier society, free from addiction and involuntary exposure to tobacco products. It promotes a comprehensive tobacco-control program involving educational, social, fiscal, and legislative interventions. It publishes several fact sheets, including *Promoting a Lethal Product* and *The Ban on Smoking on School Property: Successes and Challenges.*

Children Opposed to Smoking Tobacco (COST)
Mary Volz School, 509 W. 3rd Ave., Runnemede, NJ 08078
e-mail: costkids@costkids.org • website: www.costkids.org

COST was founded in 1996 by a group of middle school students committed to keeping tobacco products out of the hands of children. Much of the organization's efforts are spent fighting the tobacco industry's advertising campaigns directed at children and teenagers. Articles such as "Environmental Tobacco Smoke," "What Is a Parent to Do?" and "What You Can Do" are available on its website.

drkoop.com
8920 Business Park Dr., Suite 200, Austin, TX 78759
(888) 795-0998 • (512) 726-5110 • fax: (512) 726-5130
e-mail: feedback@drkoop.com • website: www.drkoop.com

Based on the vision of former U.S. surgeon general Dr. C. Everett Koop, drkoop.com is a consumer-focused interactive website that provides users with comprehensive health care information on a wide variety of subjects, including tobacco. The organization publishes reports, fact sheets, press releases, and books, including *The No-Nag, No-Guilt, Do-It-Your-Own-Way Guide to Quitting Smoking.*

Environmental Protection Agency (EPA)
Indoor Air Quality Information Clearinghouse
PO Box 37133, Washington, DC 20013-7133
(800) 438-4318 • (202) 484-1307 • fax: (202) 484-1510
e-mail: iaqinfo@aol.com • website: www.epa.gov

The EPA is the agency of the U.S. government that coordinates actions designed to protect the environment. It promotes indoor air quality standards that reduce the dangers of secondhand smoke. The EPA publishes and distributes reports such as *Respiratory Health Effects of Passive Smoking: Lung Cancer and Other Disorders* and *What You Can Do About Secondhand Smoke as Parents, Decision-Makers, and Building Occupants.*

Fight Ordinances and Restrictions to Control and Eliminate Smoking (FORCES)
PO Box 591257, San Francisco, CA 94159
(415) 824-4716
e-mail: info@forces.org • website: www.forces.org

FORCES fights against smoking ordinances and restrictions designed to eventually eliminate smoking, and it works to increase public awareness of smoking-related legislation. It opposes any state or local ordinance it feels is not fair to those who choose to smoke. Although FORCES does not advocate smoking, it asserts that an individual has the right to choose to smoke and that smokers should be accommodated wherever and whenever possible. FORCES publishes *Tobacco Weekly* as well as many articles.

Group Against Smoking Pollution (GASP)
PO Box 326, College Park, MD 20741-0632
(301) 459-4791
website: http://tobaccodocuments.org/profiles/organizations/gasp.html

Consisting of nonsmokers adversely affected by tobacco smoke, GASP works to promote the rights of nonsmokers, to educate the public about the problems of secondhand smoke, and to encourage the regulation of smoking in public places. The organization provides information and referral services and distributes educational materials, buttons, posters, and bumper stickers. GASP publishes booklets and pamphlets such as *The Nonsmokers' Bill of Rights* and *The Nonsmokers' Liberation Guide*.

KidsHealth.org
The Nemours Foundation Center for Children's Health Media
1600 Rockland Rd., Wilmington, DE 19803
(302) 651-4046 • fax: (302) 651-4077
e-mail: info@KidsHealth.org • website: www.KidsHealth.org

The mission of KidsHealth.org is to help families make informed decisions about children's health by creating the highest-quality health media. It uses cutting-edge technology and a wealth of trusted medical resources to provide the best in pediatric health information. Its teen section covers a wide variety of issues, including teen smoking. *How to Raise Non-Smoking Kids* and *Smoking: Cutting Through the Hype* are two of its numerous publications.

National Center for Tobacco-Free Kids/Campaign for Tobacco-Free Kids
1707 L St. NW, Suite 800, Washington, DC 20036
(800) 284-KIDS (284-5437)
e-mail: info@tobaccofreekids.org • website: www.tobaccofreekids.org

The National Center for Tobacco-Free Kids/Campaign for Tobacco-Free Kids is the largest private initiative ever launched to protect children from tobacco addiction. The center works in partnership with the American Cancer Society, American Heart Association, American Medical Association, the National PTA, and more than one hundred other health, civic, corporate, youth, and religious organizations. Among the center's publications are press releases, reports, and fact sheets, including *Tobacco Use Among Youth*, *Tobacco Marketing to Kids*, and *Smokeless (Spit) Tobacco and Kids*.

Bibliography

Books

Martha Work   *Stop Smoking Naturally*. Los Angeles: Keats, 2000.
Ashelman

David M. Cutler   *The Economic Impacts of the Tobacco Settlement*. Cambridge,
                    MA: National Bureau of Economic Research, 2000.

Roberta Ferrence, ed. *Nicotine and Public Health*. Washington, DC: American
                    Public Health Association, 2000.

Jonathan Gruber   *Youth Smoking in the U.S.: Evidence and Implications*. Cam-
                    bridge, MA: National Bureau of Economic Research, 2000.

Arlene B. Hirschfelder *Encyclopedia of Smoking and Tobacco*. Phoenix: Oryx,
                    1999.

Prabhat Jha and   *Tobacco Control in Developing Countries*. New York:
Frank J. Chaloupka Oxford University Press, 2000.

Judith Mackay, ed. *The Tobacco Atlas*. Geneva, Switzerland: World Health
                    Organization, 2002.

Barbara Moe   *Teen Smoking and Tobacco Use: A Hot Issue*. Springfield,
                    NJ: Enslow, 2000.

Michael J. Moore   *The Health Care Consequences of Smoking and Its Regula-
                    tion*. Cambridge, MA: National Bureau of Economic Re-
                    search, 2000.

Laury Oaks   *Smoking and Pregnancy: The Politics of Fetal Protection*.
                    New Brunswick, NJ: Rutgers University Press, 2001.

Auriana Ojeda, ed. *Smoking*. San Diego: Greenhaven Press, 2002.

Tara Parker-Pope   *Cigarettes: Anatomy of an Industry from Seed to Smoke*. New
                    York: New Press, 2001.

Robert L. Rabin, ed. *Regulating Tobacco*. New York: Oxford University Press,
                    2001.

Lesley Stern   *The Smoking Book*. Chicago: University of Chicago Press,
                    1999.

Mary E. Williams, ed. *Teen Smoking*. San Diego: Greenhaven Press, 2000.

Periodicals

Dan Alaimo   "Stung! Enforcement Stings Push Retailers to Tighten
                    Sales of Age-Restricted Products," *Supermarket News*, April
                    22, 2002.

Catherine Arnst   "The Skinny on Teen Smoking," *Business Week*, Decem-
                    ber 2, 2002.

Peter Brimelow   "The Price of Risky Behavior," *Forbes*, March 5, 2001.

Business Week   "Teen Smoking: Price Matters," March 6, 2000.

Sabra Chartrand   "Tobacco Companies Look for Ways to Reduce the
                          Smoke That Curls from a Burning Cigarette," *New York
                          Times*, November 4, 2002.

Sherri Day   "Tobacco Companies Vow to Fight $289 Billion Suit,"
                          New York Times, March 19, 2003.

Monica Dobie   "It's Curtains for Tobacco Goods," *World Tobacco*, May
                          2002.

Pial Ganguli   "Smoking in Adolescence Found to Increase Risk of Breast
                          Cancer in Women," *Practice Nurse*, November 8, 2002.

Pradeep P. Gidwani   "Television Viewing and Initiation of Smoking Among
                          Youth," *Pediatrics*, September 2002.

Greg Hewett   "Preventing Tobacco Purchases by Underage Youths,"
                          Journal of the American Medical Association, August 15,
                          2001.

Janice M. Horowitz   "Sweet as Candy, Deadly as Cigarettes: Teens Are Flock-
                          ing to a Hip Form of Smokes. There Are Hidden Dan-
                          gers," *Time*, December 16, 2002.

Marc Kaufman   "Complaints Prompt Withdrawal of Two Ads Against
                          Teen Smoking," *Washington Post*, February 16, 2000.

Cokie Lok   "Hitting Teen Smokers Where It Hurts: In the Wallet,"
                          U.S. News & World Report, August 5, 2002.

Marketing News   "JPP&M Articles Question Joe Camel's Success, Influence
                          on Teen Smoking," October 23, 2000.

Elizabeth Mayer   "Puff Test?" *New York Times*, November 22, 2002.

Karl E. Miller   "Predictors of Cigarette Smoking in Adolescents," *Ameri-
                          can Family Physician*, November 15, 2002.

Cheryl Petten   "Web Site Helps Youth Kick the Habit," *Wind Speaker*,
                          June 2001.

David Ress   "Health Agency Releases First in Series of Surveys on
                          Teen Smoking," *Business News*, January 27, 2000.

Pamela Sherrid   "Smokers' Revenge," *U.S. News & World Report*, Novem-
                          ber 4, 2002.

Steve Shive   "A Study of Young Adults Who Provide Tobacco Prod-
                          ucts to Minors," *Journal of School Health*, August 2001.

Yvonne Stephens   "A Statewide School Tobacco Policy Review: Process,
                          Results, and Implications," *Journal of School Health*, Octo-
                          ber 2002.

Julia VanTine   "Get Serious About Teen Smoking," *Prevention*, June 2000.

Peter Vilbig   "Smoked Out: Teen Cigarette Use Is Dropping. Why?
                          Credit a Combination of Advertising Restrictions, Higher
                          Prices, and the 'Truth,'" *New York Times*, May 6, 2002.

Index

362.29 TEE

Teen smoking.